Advanced Introduction to Advertising

GW00492658

Elgar Advanced Introductions are stimulating and thoughtful introductions to major fields in the social sciences, business and law, expertly written by the world's leading scholars. Designed to be accessible yet rigorous, they offer concise and lucid surveys of the substantive and policy issues associated with discrete subject areas.

The aims of the series are two-fold: to pinpoint essential principles of a particular field, and to offer insights that stimulate critical thinking. By distilling the vast and often technical corpus of information on the subject into a concise and meaningful form, the books serve as accessible introductions for undergraduate and graduate students coming to the subject for the first time. Importantly, they also develop well-informed, nuanced critiques of the field that will challenge and extend the understanding of advanced students, scholars and policy-makers.

For a full list of titles in the series please see the back of the book. Recent titles in the series include:

Employee Engagement
Alan M. Saks and Jamie A. Gruman

Governance
Jon Pierre and B. Guy Peters

Demography
Wolfgang Lutz

Environmental Compliance and Enforcement
LeRoy C. Paddock

Migration Studies
Ronald Skeldon

Landmark Criminal Cases
George P. Fletcher

Comparative Legal Methods
Pier Giuseppe Monateri

U.S. Environmental Law
E. Donald Elliott and Daniel C. Esty

Gentrification
Chris Hamnett

Family Policy
Chiara Saraceno

Law and Psychology
Tom R. Tyler

Advertising
Patrick De Pelsmacker

Advanced Introduction to

Advertising

PATRICK DE PELSMACKER
*Professor of Marketing, Faculty of Business and Economics,
University of Antwerp, Belgium*

Elgar Advanced Introductions

Cheltenham, UK • Northampton, MA, USA

Published by
Edward Elgar Publishing Limited
The Lypiatts
15 Lansdown Road
Cheltenham
Glos GL50 2JA
UK

Edward Elgar Publishing, Inc.
William Pratt House
9 Dewey Court
Northampton
Massachusetts 01060
USA

A catalogue record for this book
is available from the British Library

Library of Congress Control Number: 2021947981

ISBN 978 1 80220 088 1 (cased)
ISBN 978 1 80220 090 4 (paperback)
ISBN 978 1 80220 089 8 (eBook)

Printed and bound in Great Britain by TJ Books Limited, Padstow, Cornwall

Contents

Figures

Tables

Boxes

Preface

Advertising is everywhere, and everybody advertises. We are exposed to advertising on television, radio, in the cinema, in newspapers and magazines, on buses and in railway stations, in shops, and, of course, ubiquitously, on the Internet. Many organizations and individuals try to persuade us to think or do something. Companies want us to love and buy their products, charities want our money, social-profit organizations seek support for their good causes, be it animal rights or preservation of nature, governments urge us to obey their laws and regulations, from wearing seatbelts to adhering to Covid-19 restrictions. And of course, ordinary people like you and me help them by spreading their messages: we like, share, comment upon, and create messages following advertising on social media. We have become part of the pinball park: organizations throw in the little ball (their message) and try to keep it in the game as long as possible by stimulating the pins (us) to do so.

In six chapters, this book provides a concise yet in-depth guide to understanding, planning, and carrying out advertising, measuring its effects, and doing all that in an ethically acceptable way, all of this in a context of a media landscape that shifts from offline to online. The book tries to strike a balance between the old (but still relevant) and the new, and between theory and practice. The first chapter sets the scene: what is advertising, what is its role in businesses and organizations, and what are the implications of the offline–online shift? Chapter 2 gives an overview of the many contemporary advertising formats around. The third – and most theoretical – chapter tries to explain how advertising works. Chapter 4 discusses the various stages in the advertising planning process, and Chapter 5 goes deeper into measuring its effects. Advertising has a bad reputation, and partly rightly so. The final, and societally speaking maybe the most important, chapter digs deeper into the ethical ramifications, pitfalls, and societal consequences of current advertising practice. Apart from the many theoretical and practical insights throughout the text, a number of separate boxes go deeper into specific research insights and practical cases. Finally, the book concludes with a list of references for further reading and supplementary online resources.

Acknowledgments

In my long career as an advertising scholar, I have cooperated with many other researchers and practitioners that have been – and some of them still are – great research companions and a source of knowledge and inspiration. First of all, I should mention the long-standing cooperation with my fellow professors and good friends at the Department of Marketing of the Faculty of Business and Economics at the University of Antwerp (Belgium), my home university: Annouk Lievens, Ingrid Moons, and especially Nathalie Dens, who has been my sister-in-arms in countless advertising research projects. Next, I found great pleasure in cooperating with a number of smart, dedicated, and hard-working colleagues from other universities: Wim Janssens (who left academia), Verolien Cauberghe (Ghent University), Erlinde Cornelis (San Diego State University), Ed Malthouse (Northwestern University), Martin Eisend (European University Viadrina Frankfurt-Oder), Camilla Barbarossa (Toulouse Business School), and, last but not least, my wife Maggie Geuens (Ghent University). The majority of my research work would not have been possible without the intelligence and the dedication of many of my excellent PhD students. Thanks, Nathalia Purnawirawan, Mahdi Rajabi, Ivana Busjleta Banks, Katarina Panic, Snezha Kazakova, Yann Verhellen, Leonids Aleksandrovs, Sarah De Meulenaer, Yana Avramova, Martine Lewi, Kristien Daems, Freya De Keyzer, Ana Lopes, and Cristian Buzeta. Many thanks also for the countless advertising professionals that inspired me over the years, too many to list here, except for one, my old friend Joeri Van den Bergh (founder and co-owner of InSites Consulting), the first researcher I supervised, and long-time co-author of one of my other books. Finally, I would like to thank the Edward Elgar Publishing team for taking care of and guiding me through the process of writing this book.

1   Advertising today

Marketing communications as part of the marketing effort

According to the American Marketing Association, *marketing* is the activity, set of institutions, and processes for creating, communicating, delivering, and exchanging offerings that have value for customers, clients, partners, and society at large. Philip Kotler defines marketing as follows:

> Marketing is the science and art of exploring, creating, and delivering value to satisfy the needs of a target market at a profit. Marketing identifies unfulfilled needs and desires. It defines, measures and quantifies the size of the identified market and the profit potential. It pinpoints which segments the company is capable of serving best and it designs and promotes the appropriate products and services.[1]

Both definitions emphasize similar key concepts and tasks of marketing. It is an exchange process in which customers acquire *value* and organizations generate a commercial or social profit. From the point of view of a customer, value means the satisfaction of needs and wants. Value is usually a combination of tangible (a laptop) and intangible (using a famous brand of perfume) dimensions. The value for companies and other organizations is that marketing contributes to selling products at a profit, promotes ideas or socially desirable behaviors, or raises funds. For the marketing process to be successful, this exchange process has to be in equilibrium: the perceived value of the offer by consumers has to be at least as high as their required investment (money, time, effort …), and better than that of the competition.

What can be marketed? Anything to which the marketing logic applies: goods (cars), services (banks), events (music festivals), experiences (wellness center), people (politicians), places (New York), properties (houses), organizations (Amnesty International), information (websites), and ideas (wear your seatbelt). In marketing jargon, anything that can be marketed is referred to as a "product." These products are offered on markets: the set of actual and potential buyers of a product, and competitors that try to satisfy the same needs as the organization.

To accomplish their goals, marketers use a set of tools commonly referred to as the *marketing mix*. Traditionally, these tools are represented in the *4Ps model*: product, price, place, and promotion. Organizations have to develop products, offer them to customers at a certain price, make them available at certain places, and promote them. Each P toolbox contains specific instruments, such as branding, packaging, and extra services (Product), list prices, discounts, and credit terms (Price), retailers, locations, and logistics (Place), and sales promotions, public relations, and personal selling (Promotion). This 4Ps model has been extended with extra Ps, for instance People, Process, and Physical Evidence.

The four Ps are conceptualized from the organization's point of view: it develops products, puts a price on them, makes them available, and promotes them. A modification of this model, the *4Cs model*, takes an outside-in perspective and focuses upon customers:

- Consumer Wants and Needs: marketers should market products that people need and want;
- Cost: customers pay a price, but also have to devote time and effort to acquire a product, and often there is also an opportunity cost;
- Convenience: customers should find the products easily, and therefore they should be made available conveniently;
- Communication: marketers should create a dialogue with customers.

Advertising as part of the communication effort

Marketing communications are the means that organizations use to convey messages about their offerings to target groups with the intention to persuade them to purchase and become loyal to their products, or adopt ideas or behaviors. The marketing communications toolbox, also called the *communications mix*, is a set of tools and channels that can be used to deliver these messages and engage in two-way communications with target groups. The instruments of the communications mix include brand activation, sponsorship, public relations, point-of-sale communications, exhibitions and trade fairs, direct marketing communications, personal selling, and, of course, advertising, both offline and online.

Brand activation refers to tools such as sales promotions (e.g., buy one get one free), stimulating customer engagement (e.g., to share branded content on social media), and offering experiences (e.g., a test drive of a new car). *Sponsorship* is the support of a person or organization, in cash or kind (e.g., goods, services, know-how), in return for exploitable marketing benefits for the sponsoring company, such as building brand awareness, improving brand image, stimulating product trial, or acquiring new customers. *Public relations* are communications of a company with its audiences or stakeholders, groups of individuals or organizations with whom the company wants to create goodwill (e.g., media, retailers, communication agencies, banks, …). *Point-of-sale communications* is communication at or near the point of sale (e.g., displays, product presentation in the shop, store layout). *Exhibitions and trade fairs* are, particularly in business-to-business and industrial markets, used for contacting and meeting prospects, users and purchasers. *Direct marketing communications* are a personal and direct way to communicate with customers and potential clients or prospects (e.g., direct mailings, email campaigns, telemarketing). *Personal selling* is face-to-face selling in which a salesperson tries to convince the customer to buy a product.

And then there is *advertising*. The definition of advertising by the American Marketing Association is any paid form of non-personal presentation and promotion of ideas, goods, and services by an identified sponsor. The American Advertising Academy defines advertising as a (usually) paid for and mediated form of communication from an identifiable source, designed to inform and persuade the receiver to take some action, now or in the future. One other definition is: "Advertising consists of all the activities involved in presenting to a group a non-personal, oral or visual, openly sponsored message regarding a product, service or idea. This message, called an advertisement, is disseminated through one or more media and is paid for by the identified sponsor."[2]

Most of these definitions include a number of common features of advertising. However, some of these do not reflect today's advertising practices. First of all, advertising is said to be (mostly) paid for by an identified sponsor: someone has paid for the advertisement, and the person who is exposed to the ad is aware of that. When seeing a television ad or a billboard featuring a brand, most consumers will understand that the brand has paid for the ads. However, contemporary advertising formats are often hybrid, and try to "hide" the commercial message in other content (for instance, by means of brand placement in movies) such that consumers might not be aware of the message's commercial intentions. Also, in the broad sense of the word, when social media users share branded content on these platforms (called "earned media" resulting in "organic reach," see hereafter), that can indirectly also be regarded as advertising. Indeed, other social media users are exposed to the message that, moreover, was not paid for, since it was spread by other consumers for free. Another common feature of most definitions is that advertising is mediated; in other words, it uses different kinds of media channels (e.g., television, newspapers, outdoor, websites …) to reach the intended target groups. That qualifies advertising as a mass media communication tool.

Another common focus of all definitions is that advertising is not only used to sell products, but intends to inform, persuade and activate people. Indeed, advertising often does not lead to an immediate sales effect. Often, by means of advertising, people are guided through what is called the sales funnel (see hereafter): prospective customers should be made aware of a brand or a product, should acquire knowledge about the product, develop a positive attitude toward a brand, develop an interest in it, and the intention to try it, and make them visit a shop to check things out further (activation). Advertising works on information and persuasion that eventually should lead to conversion of potential prospects into actual customers and sales.

One last aspect that several definitions have in common is that advertising is qualified as a non-personal form of communication, because it is basically a monologue via mass media: the brand sends the same message to a lot of consumers who cannot respond or interact with the brand. However, in the context of online advertising, one of the key features of advertising is personalization or customization, the ability to proactively tailor advertising messages to characteristics and tastes of individual consumers, by combining the use of technology and customer information to tailor communication interactions between a business and each individual customer. Online advertising aims at delivering the right message at the right time to the right person. That increasingly makes contemporary online advertising both a massive, but also an interactive and personal, communication tool.

Additionally, the lines between what could be called advertising and what are considered other instruments of the communication mix are increasingly blurred. For instance, brand placement in other media content (e.g., movies, games …) can be considered advertising: there is a commercial intent to inform and persuade (potential) customers, it uses mass media (e.g., movies, television shows, books, games) to do so, and in principle there is an identified sponsor (or there should be). Similarly, influencer marketing, the promotion of brands by social media influencers, can be considered advertising for the same reasons. Despite the fact that some would call brand placement or influencer marketing sponsorship of media content, for all practical purposes, it is advertising. Formats such as content marketing, storytelling and buzz marketing, although (partly) borrowed from other disciplines such as public relations (PR), can be considered advertising since they are indeed intended to influence (potential) consumers' knowledge, attitudes, and behaviors toward products via mass media messages. Indirectly, a branded and paid post on social media that is shared by a user of these media is advertising since it is a communication consequence of company-initiated advertising.

For the purpose of this book, I define advertising as follows: "Advertising is any (mostly) paid and mediated form of promotion of products, brands, companies or ideas in offline or online mass media by an identified source, designed to inform and persuade target groups and/or stimulate them to take some action, now or in the future."

Most communication campaigns do not only use different advertising media and channels, but also other instruments of the communication mix to reach out to consumers. Nowadays, marketers try to reach (potential) consumers by means of as many "touch points" as possible. This is called 360-degree communications. Additionally, whether a campaign uses few or many channels and instruments, there is always the need for integrated marketing communications (IMC). IMC is "consistency across communications channels and over time." It means linking all promotion tools to work together in harmony. Potential consumers do not distinguish between the different tools and instruments of the marketing communications mix. To them, all communications by a brand are perceived as persuasion attempts, regardless of whether it is a banner on the Internet, a television ad, or a billboard along a soccer field. They thus consider all these stimuli as brand messages from undistinguishable sources. Therefore, all instruments and channels of a communications campaign should be consistent in terms of message content and message style. The message receivers should perceive all these stimuli as coming from the same brand conveying the same basic message and brand position. IMC is speaking with one voice, all the time.

A second important principle of IMC is synergy. Campaigns will be more effective if they are mutually reinforcing: the effects of all tools taken together will then be stronger than the sum of each separate tool. In the current 360-degree communications context, creating synergy becomes increasingly imperative and complicated. Synergy can take many forms. The work of a salesperson can be much easier if the company also uses advertising to create awareness and favorable attitudes toward the company's products. A sales promotion campaign will probably be more effective if accompanied by an advertising campaign. Sponsorship effects can be reinforced by advertising campaigns. Online campaigns and offline campaigns can be combined for a better effect. All this means that advertising is not a standalone instrument. It has to be consistently and synergistically integrated in the whole communications campaign.

Advertising in the digital age

Offline mass marketing communications media and techniques have dominated communications strategies for decades. However, people's media consumption has increasingly shifted toward the online world. Global Internet penetration rates range (at the end of 2020) from 46.2% in Africa, 62.6% in Asia, around 70% in Latin America and the Middle East, to almost 90% in North America and Europe.[3] People also increasingly spend more time on digital media, both in absolute terms and as a part of total media use. Total media use (including multi-tasking and multi-screening) was about 7 hours per day in 2011, 7.5 hours in 2016, and more than 8 hours projected in 2021. In 2011, Internet use was 17.9% of all media use, in 2016 it was 29.5%, and in 2021 it is projected to be 38.8%. Moreover, *mobile* device use as a percentage of Internet use has increased spectacularly, from 42.7% in 2011 to 70.1% in 2016, and a projected 80.7% in 2021. This means that, in 2021, mobile accounts for a projected media use of more than 30% of all media use.[4] Nevertheless, traditional offline media, largely television, also remain important.

Another remarkable phenomenon is the importance of social media use in people's lives. *Social media* are websites and other online means of communication that are used by large groups of people to share information and to develop social and professional contacts.[5] Social media usage is booming. In 2017, there were 2.86 billion active social media users, a number that increased to 3.60 billion in 2020, and is projected to further increase to 4.41 billion in 2025.[6] In January 2021, Facebook holds the lead with 2.74 billion active users, followed by YouTube (2.29 billion), WhatsApp (2 billion), Messenger (1.30 billion), Instagram (1.22 billion), Weixin/WeChat (1.21 billion), and TikTok (0.69 billion).[7] On average, in 2020, global Internet users spent 2 hours and 22 minutes on social media per day (though trends differed widely by country[8]) an increase of one hour a day since 2012.[9] Moreover, most social media use is mobile. Consequently, social media are one of the most important channels to communicate with consumers.

Not only do people spend a lot of time on social media, but a substantial part of them use these media to actively look for product and brand information. In a 2019 study, 31% of social media users reported that their main motivation in using social media was to research and find products to buy,[10] 40% of Internet users said they followed their favorite brands on social media, and 37% of online shoppers said that they looked for inspiration on social media before they shopped.[11] Consequently, not only can advertisers find "eyeballs" on social media, but they can also reach an interested and captive audience by using these channels. The total spending on advertising worldwide has increased steadily over the years. It is estimated at $718.21 billion in 2020 and is expected to grow to $822.39 billion in 2024. In 2018, digital ad spending was $283.35 billion (45.9% of total spend), increasing to $384.96 billion in 2020 (53.6%), and expected to grow to $517.51 billion (60.5%) in 2023. In 2019, advertising on Google represented 31.1% of all digital ad spend, followed by Facebook with 20.2%.[12] Thus, not only are digital advertising budgets growing, but also their share of total advertising spend. Nevertheless, television advertising remains very important. In 2019, worldwide, 33.6% of total budgets was spent on television advertising.[13] Mobile advertising spend is increasing rapidly. In 2019, it amounted to $189 billion, and it is expected to surpass $240 billion by 2022. This means that, in 2022, mobile advertising's share of total worldwide ad spending would be one third of all advertising budgets, and more than half of all digital advertising.[14] Table 1.1 shows total ad spend and forecast spend in Western Europe (2017–22) and the market shares of media types. The steady annual growth of total ad spend slowed during the Covid-19 year 2020, but is projected to pick up again from 2021 onward. Online advertising market shares show a yearly increase to more than 50% from 2020 onward. Outdoor, radio, and cinema are more or less maintaining their (low) market share, while television and especially newspapers and magazines are losing ground year after year.

Advertising in a cross-cultural environment

More and more companies are operating internationally. International advertising has to operate in different environments with different

Table 1.1   Total ad spend (Mln€) per year and market share of media types in Western Europe (%)

Medium	2017	2018	2019	2020*	2021*	2022*
Internet	40.01	44.18	47.88	50.21	50.86	51.94
Television	26.89	25.62	24.10	24.33	23.76	23.31
Newspapers	13.13	11.34	10.09	9.21	8.91	8.49
Magazines	7.76	6.90	6.05	5.59	5.27	4.91
Outdoor	6.46	6.44	6.46	5.61	6.01	6.07
Radio	5.04	4.86	4.70	4.57	4.56	4.53
Cinema	0.71	0.66	0.72	0.48	0.63	0.75
Total ad spend (Mln€)	86,453	91,087	91,229	80,124	86,773	90,152

Note: * figures are forecasts.
Source: Based on data from https://www.statista.com/statistics/799801/ad-spend-in-western-europe-media/.

demographic, economic, geographic, technological, political, legal, and especially cultural conditions. Besides different regulations regarding advertising instruments, media availability and the popularity of different media, cultural phenomena can have a major impact on international advertising campaigns. *Culture* is the collective programming of the mind which distinguishes the members of one group or category of people from those of another. In order to succeed in international marketing and advertising, professionals have to understand these cultural differences since consumers adhere to certain values and beliefs, and will therefore respond differently to advertising. International advertisers have to understand other cultures and take them into account in their campaigns.

There are a number of important components of culture that may have an impact on how advertising messages are perceived. First, there is verbal language. Subtle differences or different pronunciations may convey totally different meanings. For instance, in Asian countries such as Japan and Thailand, language differs according to who is speaking. In Japan, the level of formality of the language depends on the gender and the status of the speaker. For marketing communications, this means that the seller always has to place him- or herself in an inferior position. Furthermore, translation of words may lead to more space requirements, which can alter the overall layout of the ad. Also, non-verbal language is important. Non-verbal language includes timing, spatial orientation, gestures, touch, colors, and eye contact. Further, perceptions of time may be different. Is time money or do people consider it to be indefinitely available? A time-is-money person (such as in Europe and the U.S.A.) may find an ad that appeals to "saving time" convincing, in contrast to people who do not adhere to this time concept. Also, a distinction can be made between a time orientation toward the past, present, or future. Many European countries have an orientation toward the past, using the past to explain where they are now. Americans are more future-orientated, while Muslim countries are usually rather fatalistic and adhere to a present-time orientation. For instance, history-related advertising appeals may not work so well in the U.S.A.

There are also space-related issues. According to Hall's "proxemics," Western countries are characterized by three primary zones of space: the intimate zone (0–45 cm), the personal zone (45 cm–1 m) and the social zone (1–2 m). These zones can be different in other parts of the world. Northern Europeans, the English, and Americans are said to have a low-touch culture, demonstrating low contact in public, while Southern Europeans, Arabs, and Eastern Europeans are said to have a high-touch culture. Colors have different meanings in different cultures. For instance, in the U.S.A. and Europe, green is often associated with freshness, the environment, and good health, but in countries with dense green jungles it is associated with disease instead. Red suggests good fortune in China but means death in Turkey. White stands for purity and cleanliness in many European countries, but suggests death in many Asian countries. Cultures also differ in the way they greet each other: shaking hands, bowing, kissing, and so on. Patting a child on the head is a sign of affection in Western cultures, but an insult in Islamic countries. Looking someone straight in the eye is regarded positively by Europeans and Americans because it is perceived as a sign of honesty. However, in Japan you show respect by lowering your eyes.

Religion influences what is allowed to be said or shown in an advertising message. For example, in France in 1998, Volkswagen had to withdraw its billboards for the new Golf since it was said to mock the Last Supper. Secondly, religion influences the value people attach to material goods. According to Islam and Buddhism, material wealth is immoral, while in the Western world wealth is a symbol of achievement. Therefore, status appeals can be expected to be more successful in Western countries than in Islamic or Buddhist countries. Thirdly, religion has an influence on what products can and cannot be consumed.

Gender roles differ from one country to another. In some countries, in advertising, women are expected to be depicted in the home taking care of the children. In others, women are concerned with looking beautiful or are often shown in white-collar and service occupations. In some countries, advertising sticks much more to traditional gender roles than in others. Using traditional gender roles in advertising may be advisable in some countries, but not done in others.

Another relevant factor for advertising is the difference between high- and low-context cultures. A high-context communication or message is one in which most of the information is either in the physical context or internalized in the person, while very little is in the coded, explicit, transmitted part of the message. A low-context communication is just the opposite; that is, the mass of the information is vested in the explicit code. In other words, in *low-context cultures*, a lot of emphasis is placed on words. One is as accurate, explicit, and unambiguous as possible so that the receiver can easily decode the message and understand what is meant. In *high-context cultures* words are one part of the message; the other part is formed by body language and the context, that is, the social setting, and the importance and knowledge of the person. In the latter case, the message is more ambiguous and implicit. For example, Japanese ads have been shown to contain fewer information cues, less emphasis on the product's benefits, fewer comparisons, and to consist of more emotional appeals than American ads. In other words, in Japan a soft sell approach is preferred, while in the U.S.A. a hard sell approach is more frequently encountered.

Cultural values

According to Hofstede, six cultural value dimensions can be distinguished which can explain the differences in culture across countries (Figure 1.1). In *individualist cultures* there are loose ties between people and they look after themselves and their immediate family only. In *collectivistic cultures* people belong to strong, cohesive in-groups who look after and protect each other in exchange for unquestioning loyalty. Central to individualism is giving priority to personal goals over the goals of the group, as well as an emphasis on differentiation and achievement, while collectivism stands for the reverse: harmony, conformism, group goals, participation, and teamwork above all. This leads to differences in advertising appreciation.

Power distance refers to the extent to which authority plays an important role, and to what extent less powerful members of the society accept and expect that power is distributed unequally. In high-power-distance cultures, a few people have all the power and make all the decisions; the other people carry out orders. In low-power-distance cultures, power is not concentrated in the hands of a few and interactions between people occur on a more equal basis. For advertising, this might mean that expert endorsers are more appropriate in high-power-distance cultures in which people are used to being and expect to be told what to do, while information-dense ads might be more appropriate in low-power-distance cultures in which people appreciate making decisions on the basis of information offered. In *masculine cultures*, assertiveness, competitiveness, achievement, heroism,

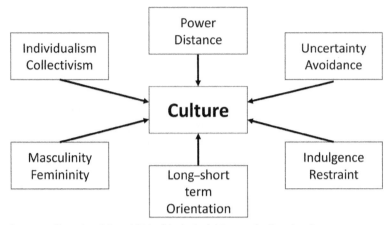

Source: Based on https://hi.hofstede-insights.com/national-culture.

Figure 1.1   Hofstede's six dimensions of cultural values

status, and material rewards for success are valued highly, while in *feminine cultures*, caring for others, a preference for cooperation, modesty, caring for the weak, and quality of life are central values. This can have a great impact on how, for instance, traditional stereotypical advertising messages will be appreciated (or not) (Box 1.1).

Box 1.1   Research: a cross-cultural analysis of male and female gender role stereotyping in advertising

Gender role stereotypes refer to beliefs about the psychological traits, behaviors, and occupational status that are regarded as differentially appropriate for men or women. An empirical study compared responses to male and female gender role stereotypes in Sweden and Germany, two countries that vary substantially in their cultural background. In comparison with the Swedish, Germans score higher on cultural values such as masculinity, power distance, and assertiveness values. The study was based on a 3 (degree of gender stereotyping: counter-stereotypical, neutral, stereotypical) × 2 (model gender: male, female) between-subjects experiment. An unknown brand of soda was selected as the advertised product. The questionnaire was provided in

Swedish to Swedish participants (n = 507) and in German to German participants (n = 506). In each country, respondents were randomly exposed to one of the six test advertisements, and completed a number of online questions on the advertisement, the brand, and their cultural values.

Overall, consumers responded more positively to ads with higher perceived degrees of stereotyping, especially for male role portrayals. Responses to stereotyping become more favorable with increasing degrees of masculinity and power distance. For high-assertiveness individuals the gender of the model influences ad and brand attitudes, while this is not the case for low-assertiveness individuals. High-assertiveness individuals have better ad and brand attitudes toward a higher degree of stereotyping for male role portrayals and a lower degree of stereotyping for female role portrayals. Since high-assertiveness individuals stress equity, competition, and performance, high-assertiveness individuals could prefer men and women in a working setting, instead of a domestic setting, since a working setting stresses competition and a "can-do" attitude.

Uncertainty avoidance refers to the degree to which members of a society feel uncomfortable with uncertainty and ambiguity and have a need for structure and formal rules in their lives. High uncertainty avoidance cultures maintain rigid codes of belief and behavior, and are intolerant of unorthodox behavior and ideas. Weak uncertainty avoidance societies maintain a more relaxed attitude in which practice counts more than principles. Advertising for uncertainty avoidance cultures can focus on expert appeals and provide information and guarantees to reassure consumers. Societies prioritize either a *long-term versus short-term orientation*. Societies that are short-term oriented prefer to maintain time-honored traditions and norms while viewing societal change with suspicion. Long-term oriented cultures, on the other hand, take a more pragmatic approach: they encourage thrift and efforts in modern education as a way to prepare for the future. Finally, there is the *indulgence–restraint* dimension. Indulgence stands for a society that allows relatively free gratification of basic and natural human drives related to enjoying life and having fun. Restraint stands for a society that suppresses gratification of needs and regulates it by means of strict social norms. It goes without saying that these two latter dimensions will also be of great influence on how advertising appeals persuade consumers or not.

Standardization or adaptation

Once a company decides to go international, one of the most important strategic decisions to be made is to what extent to follow a global or cross-culturally standardized strategy or a local adapted one. A *standardized (globalized) campaign* is one that is run in different countries, using the same concept, setting, theme, appeal, and message, with the possible exception of translations. A local approach (*localization or adaptation*) implies that most elements of the communications strategy are adapted to local circumstances. *Globalization* of advertising generally leads to cost reduction through economies of scale. Global campaigns offer the advantage of globally exploiting a great creative idea and make things simpler for the company in the sense that coordination and control of the advertising program in different countries become easier. Moreover, a global image can be created across different parts of the world. Brands that have advertised globally include Nivea, Martini, L'Oréal, Xerox, and Parker pens. Additionally, globalized advertising can help to create a strong global brand identity. The perception of brand globalness is often associated with prestige and quality, which benefits purchase intention.

However, the differences between nations' and consumers' cultures around the world do not guarantee that the same ad can be similarly effective in all the countries. People living in different cultures differ in their beliefs, previous experiences, attitudes, values, and so on. Different values might lead to different needs, different consumption behavior, and different ways to persuade consumers by means of advertising. Localizing an advertisement often increases self-brand congruity, which makes the ad and the brand more appealing to local consumers. Often, the best way to approach international markets is not to adhere to one of the extreme strategies of globalization or localization, but to opt for a "global commitment to a local vision," or in other words to "think global, but act local" (*glocalization*). If the brand positioning is a good one, the brand should be rolled out in most countries. Also, an excellent creative idea can work nearly everywhere. However, even the best ideas might need some adaptation in execution to get into the mindset of local people or to respect their cultural values. One example would be to work out a global creative idea, but to adapt the advertising so that local presenters, experts, or celebrities are employed, or that reference is made to local history or national symbols: Big Ben in London, the Eiffel Tower in Paris, the Atomium in Brussels, the gondolas in Venice. Glocalized advertising campaigns often combine global elements, such as a global brand name and positioning, with local elements, such as wording or a local celebrity endorser.

Box 1.2   Research: openness to foreign markets and advertising adaptation

Through an online survey, 405 respondents from three countries, Belgium (136), India (131), and Iran (138), were randomly assigned to one of three advertising strategies. In each country, three different ads were prepared for a fictitious brand of home cinema systems (TFX), manipulated by two executional elements, i.e. the celebrity endorser and advertising copy. Both elements were either fully adapted (local celebrity and advertising copy) to the context of the three nations or standardized (international celebrity and advertising copy). In addition, a glocalization strategy was created by combining a local celebrity with an international advertising copy. To manipulate the advertising copy, the language, the location, and the website domain were locally adapted or internationally standardized. The international advertising copy was drafted in English, mentioning three international metropolitan cities and referring to a website "tfx.com." The localized advertising copy was in Hindi for India, in Farsi for Iran, and in Dutch for Belgium, naming three metropolitan cities of each country (e.g., for India: Delhi, Mumbai, and Kolkota), and referring to websites with adapted domains of each country (e.g., for India: "tfx.in").

The three countries have different levels of openness to foreign markets. To measure a nation's openness to foreign markets, the KOF index of globalization was used. The KOF index measures the social, cultural, economic, and political openness of a country. It scores countries on a 0–100 scale. On the basis of these scores, in 2017, Belgium was extremely open to foreign markets (KOF = 91.61, rank 2nd/191); India scores a moderate 50.41 (rank 112th/191); Iran has a low KOF score of 41.27 (rank 156th/191).

The results of the study show the following. Societies with low openness to foreign markets such as Iran consider foreign values and norms as perceptually distant. In these societies, ads with international elements, either glocalized or standardized, are less positively received than completely adapted ad appeals. In societies with a moderate openness to foreign markets such as India, individuals have some contact with foreign cultures, but also evaluate ads on the basis of their congruency with their own local culture. As a result, advertising requires at least a link to the local culture, through glocalization or complete adaptation. In these countries, standardization of advertising is a suboptimal strategy, but full adaptation is not necessary. In societies with a high openness to foreign markets such as Belgium, individuals have frequent contact with the norms and values of other cultures. In those countries consumer responses do not differ significantly between advertisement strategies. The results of the study show that glocalization is as effective in moderately to highly open countries, while full standardization can be equally effective for a nation with high level of openness to foreign markets.

Some product categories seem to lend themselves better to a global approach than others. For instance, some products can be sold to similar target groups that share similar opinions, values, interests, and so on across countries. Young people or people with a higher education, for example, are very similar, whether they are French, Italian, German, Belgian, or American. These groups, in general, are more open-minded, less culturally bound, more receptive to international media, make more use of international media, and have more international contacts and/or go abroad more often. This factor explains the success of, for instance, Calvin Klein and Apple. Images, visual messages, and international music lend themselves more to standardization than a spoken or written message. Examples of successful campaigns in this category are Levi's, Coca-Cola, Martini, Smirnoff vodka, perfume ads, and airline campaigns. Luxury products are targeted at upper-class people who buy the product for the status it brings. Because only the status and no product information needs to be communicated, these appeals are easier to standardize. Innovative, high-tech products, such as the latest computers or software, seem to be used everywhere in the same way, which can justify a global appeal. Products with a country-of-origin appeal can be more easily globalized. For instance, Belgium and Switzerland are famous for their chocolate, France and Italy for their wine, Japan for its technology, Germany for its cars, and Switzerland for its watches. Products that use a country-of-origin positioning may well be advertised by means of a global approach.

Notes

1. https://www.kotlermarketing.com/phil_questions.shtml.
2. https://www.economicsdiscussion.net/advertising/definitions-of-advertising/31793.
3. https://www.internetworldstats.com/stats.htm.
4. https://www.statista.com/statistics/256300/time-spent-with-media-worldwide/#:~:text=The%20statistic%20presents%20data%20on,minutes%20per%20day%20in%202021; https://www.statista.com/statistics/319732/daily-time-spent-online-device/.
5. https://www.dictionary.com/browse/social-media.
6. https://www.statista.com/statistics/278414/number-of-worldwide-social-network-users/.
7. https://www.statista.com/statistics/272014/global-social-networks-ranked-by-number-of-users/.
8. https://www.statista.com/chart/18983/time-spent-on-social-media/#:~:text=On%20average%20global%20internet%20users,trends%20differed%20widely%20by%20country.
9. https://www.broadbandsearch.net/blog/average-daily-time-on-social-media.
10. http://www.globalwebindex.com.
11. https://www.wordstream.com/blog/ws/2018/07/19/advertising-statistics.
12. https://www.emarketer.com/content/global-digital-ad-spending-2019.
13. https://www.statista.com/topics/5952/television-advertising-worldwide/.
14. https://www.statista.com/statistics/303817/mobile-internet-advertising-revenue-worldwide/#:~:text=In%202019%2C%20mobile%20advertising%20spending,by%20the%20end%20of%202022.

2 Advertising formats

Types of advertising and appeals

Different types of advertising can be distinguished (Table 2.1). Advertising can be defined on the basis of the sender of the message. Manufacturer advertising is initiated by a manufacturing company that promotes its own brands. Collective advertising takes place when a government or public agent takes the initiative. Retail organizations (for instance supermarkets) also advertise. Sometimes two manufacturing companies, or a retailer and a manufacturer, jointly develop an advertising campaign. This is called cooperative advertising. Besides goods and services, ideas can be promoted, mostly by not-for-profit organizations (e.g., wear your seatbelt, support animal welfare).

Table 2.1   Types of advertising

Sender	*Message*
Manufacturer	Informational
Collective	Transformational
Retailer	Institutional
Cooperative	Selective vs. generic
Idea	Theme vs. action
Receiver	*Media*
Consumer	Audio-visual
Industry	Print
Trade	
Stakeholders	
Offline vs. online	*Appeals*
	Rational
	Emotional
	Endorsers

The intended receiver of the advertising message can be either a private end-consumer or another company. In the latter case, the company may buy the products to use in its own production process (industrial advertising), or buy the products to resell them (trade advertising). Advertising can also be targeted at stakeholders other than customers (e.g., suppliers, banks, governments, investors) in the context of corporate communications that is aimed at establishing and maintaining the corporate reputation. Different types of advertising can also be distinguished according to the type of message conveyed. Informational advertising tries to appeal to informational buying consumer motives such as solving or avoiding a problem, or normal stock depletion (e.g., detergents, diapers, insurance). Transformational advertising appeals to transformational consumer motives, such as sensory gratification, social approval, or intellectual stimulation (e.g., ice cream, nice cars, books). Institutional advertising is the term used to describe government campaigns. Selective advertising campaigns try to promote a specific brand, while a generic advertising campaign promotes a whole product category, such as French wine or Italian fashion. Theme advertising attempts to build awareness and positive attitudes toward a brand or a product. Action advertising tries to activate consumers, for instance to visit a store or a website or to buy a product. Finally, different types of campaigns can be distinguished on the basis of the type of medium in which the ad is placed, such as audio-visual (e.g., television or radio) and print (e.g., newspapers or magazines).

Advertising agencies or creatives can use a multitude of appeals, formats, and execution strategies to express or translate their creative idea. Two main types of creative appeals can be distinguished: rational appeals and emotional appeals. *Rational advertising appeals* contain features, practical details, and verifiable, factually relevant cues that can serve as evaluative criteria. *Emotional advertising appeals* are advertisements whose main purpose is to elicit affective responses. Mixed appeals employ both rational and emotional elements. For both emotional and rational appeals, different formats or execution strategies and different types of endorsers can be used (Table 2.2). Several of the formats that can be used for rational appeals could just as well be used for emotional appeals, although they are discussed here only once. For example, a comparative ad can be purely factual, describing own and competitive prices, but could also be humorous, such as Virgin's campaign featuring large billboards in airports with the message "Enjoy your overpriced flight."

Table 2.2   Advertising appeals

Rational appeals	Emotional appeals
Talking head	Humor
Demonstration	Eroticism
Problem solution	Warmth
Testimonial	Fear
Slice of life	Shock tactics
Dramatization	
Comparative ads	

Endorsers
Experts
Celebrities
Influencers

Rational appeals

Rational ads may contain one or several information cues, such as price, quality, performance, components, availability, special offers, taste, nutrition, warranties, research results, new ideas, and safety. A *talking head* format is an ad in which the characters tell a story in their own words. Usually these formats have a problem–solution structure. In a *demonstration*, consumers are shown how a product works, focusing on product attributes and/or benefits and product uses while demonstrating the product. For example, when the brand Febreze was launched in Europe, ads showed consumers that the product could be used for preventing disturbing odors in clothes, sofas, curtains, cars, and so on. A *problem solution* ad shows how a problem can be solved or avoided. For example, the ads for Head & Shoulders feature an elegant-looking business professional wearing a nice dark suit. Unfortunately, he has a dandruff problem which clearly shows on the suit: Head & Shoulders can solve this problem. A *testimonial* features ordinary people saying how good a product is. Typical products which are advertised in this way are detergents: "I really was amazed; my clothes have never been so white." Testimonials are often effective because they rely on the positive membership reference group effect: people like to take other people that have had and solved similar problems as an example and inspiration. *Slice-of-life* ads feature the product being used in a real-life setting that the target group can relate to, which usually involves solving a problem. *Dramatization advertising* is rather similar to a slice of life. Both first present a problem and afterward the solution, but a dramatization builds suspense and leads consumers to a climax. *Comparative advertising* can be used as a means to differentiate a brand from a competitor. A direct comparative ad explicitly names the comparison brand (often a well-known competitive brand) and claims that the comparison brand is inferior to the advertised brand with respect to a specific attribute. An indirect comparative ad does not explicitly mention a comparison brand, but argues to be superior on a certain attribute compared with other brands ("Gillette, the best a man can get").

Emotional appeals

Emotional advertising tries to evoke emotions in consumers rather than to make them think. Emotional ads mainly consist of non-verbal elements such as images and emotional stimuli. *Humorous advertising* is an appeal created with the intent to make people laugh. Humor in advertising has been studied by many researchers, and overall there is only one aspect on which agreement can be found: humor attracts attention. However, there may be a distraction effect in that humorous advertising attracts attention to the ad, but not necessarily to the brand. Humorous advertising appears to be more appropriate for low- than for high-involvement products, and in situations where consumers are affectively ("feel") rather than cognitively ("think") motivated. Consequently, humor should be avoided for high-involvement/cognitive products, such as banking and insurance, and is expected to work better for low-involvement/affective products such as ice cream and cookies. In general, humor seems to be more effective for existing and familiar brands than for new and unfamiliar brands, and humor that is related to the product is more effective than unrelated humor. Finally, humor may have a detrimental effect when prior brand evaluations are negative. In other words, if you are convinced that a Lion bar tastes awful and sticks to your teeth, you are more likely to think that the company wants to be funny, but is not funny at all, while a positive brand attitude leads to more tolerance and acceptance of humorous advertising.

An ad is erotic if it uses nudity, physical contact between two adults, sexy or provocatively dressed person(s), provocative or seductive facial expression, and suggestive words or sexually laden music. *Erotic advertising* attracts attention, albeit not always to the brand or the message. Indeed, many studies show that eroticism reduces brand and message recall. Another negative aspect on which most researchers agree is that eroticism has a negative impact on the image of the advertiser. The more intense the eroticism or, in other words, the more overt the sex appeal, the more negative the responses to the ad become. The more the erotic appeal is related to the product, the more positive the responses to it become. In other words, functional products such as underwear, bath foam or shower cream, and romantic products such as perfume, aftershave, alcohol, or cosmetics are expected to benefit more from an erotic appeal than other product categories such as coffee or a lawnmower. *Warm advertising* contains elements that evoke mild, positive feelings such as love, friendship, coziness, affection, and empathy. Although mixed results have been reported as to the effect of warmth on message and brand recall and recognition, warmth leads to more positive affective responses, less negative feelings such as irritation, a more positive attitude toward the ad and toward the brand, and sometimes an enhanced purchase intention.

Fear appeal advertising (or threat-based advertising) shows a certain type of risk (threat) that a person might be exposed to and which she usually can reduce by buying a product (e.g., insurance) or not buying one or acting in a certain way (e.g., not drinking when driving). Risks that might be used in fear appeal are physical (bodily harm, often used for burglar alarms, toothpaste, analgesics), social (being socially ostracized, often used for deodorants, dandruff shampoo, mouthwash), time (spending a lot of time on an unpleasant activity while the activity can be performed in less time; for instance, when introducing dishwashers, messages such as "Do you realize that most people spend X years of their life washing the dishes?"), product performance (competitive brands do not perform adequately; Dyson vacuum cleaners are promoted as having no bag, which makes them the only cleaner to maintain 100% suction, 100% of the time), financial (losing a lot of money, typically used by insurance companies), and opportunity loss (missing a special opportunity if they do not act right away; e.g., the Belgian mobile phone provider Proximus ran a campaign with the message: "Subscribe now to Proximus, and pay nothing until April"). Research shows that threat appeals are capable of sensitizing people to threats and of changing their behavior (Box 2.1).

Box 2.1   Research: how fear appeals work

Fear or threat appeals are persuasive messages designed to scare people by describing the terrible things that will happen to them if they do not do what the message recommends. Threat appeals are often used as persuasive messages in public service announcements or social profit campaigns, for instance anti-smoking, HIV, speeding, drunk driving, but also commercial companies such as banks and insurance companies occasionally use threat appeals. The objective is to increase the involvement of people with an issue or a problem by presenting it as threatening, and to offer a credible solution, such as the adaptation of a certain behavior, or purchasing a certain brand. Several mechanisms for how fear appeals work have been proposed.

"Drive models" claim that moderate levels of fear appeals work best: some fear is needed to motivate people to reach a negative drive state. However, the fear has to be able to be reduced (drive reduction). If fear is too high, maladaptive behavior will follow as a result of "reactance," the motivation to resist any perceived threat to one's freedom to make up one's own mind about an issue. The Protection Motivation Theory (PMT), on the other hand, prescribes that four independent cognitive responses mediate the impact of a threat appeal on coping attitudes, intentions, and behavior: perceived severity, an individual's beliefs about the seriousness of the threat; perceived susceptibility or probability of occurrence, an individual's beliefs about his or her chances of experiencing the threat; perceived response efficacy, an individual's beliefs as to whether a response effectively prevents the threat; and perceived self-efficacy, an individual's belief in his or her ability to perform the recommended response. Perceived severity and susceptibility represent the perceived level of threat; perceived response efficacy and self-efficacy represent the perceived level of efficacy to do something about the threat. Threat messages consequently lead to protection motivation which, in turn, has an impact on attitudes and coping intention and behavior.

The Extended Parallel Processing Model defines two reactions to threat appeals: a mainly cognitive one (danger control), where people think about the threat and ways to avert it; and a mainly emotional one (fear control), in which people react to their fear and engage in strategies (reactance, defensive avoidance) to control their fear. Too high levels of evoked fear may lead to fear control and thus to ineffective messages. High levels of threat (caused by or inducing fear), combined with high levels of coping efficacy perception ("I can do something about it"), lead to danger control and message acceptance: people feel threatened, but have the impression that they can do something about it. On the other hand, high levels of threat combined with low levels of perceived coping efficacy lead to fear control and message rejection. People feel threatened and get the impression that they cannot do anything about it, and hence ignore or reject the message.

Shock advertising deliberately startles and offends an audience because it violates norms, transgresses laws or customs (e.g., indecent sexual reference, obscenity), or breaches a social or moral code (e.g., vulgarity, gratuitous violence, disgusting images). Examples are the Benetton ads showing a nun kissing a priest or a man dying of AIDS. The main advantage of these tactics is that they secure the audience's attention. Recipients of these messages usually also engage in more cognitive elaboration because they want to figure out what the message is all about. Moreover, shock ads often generate (online) word-of-mouth and media publicity, thereby increasing their reach and impact.

Endorsers

Besides testimonials of consumers, in advertising, a brand, product, or claim can be endorsed by experts, celebrities, or influencers. *Experts* can be used to demonstrate the quality or high technology of a product. For example, toothpaste brands are often promoted by means of someone in a white lab coat to imply a dentist's opinion. The effectiveness of this type of ad is assumed to be based on the perceived credibility of the expert's judgment. Celebrities can also be used to endorse a product. Their effectiveness is based on the "aspiration group" effect. Examples of *celebrity endorsement* are George Clooney for Nescafé, LeBron James for Nike, and Rihanna for Puma. Several studies have shown that celebrities can have a direct positive impact on ad likeability and also an indirect effect on brand attitude and purchase intentions. According to the *Source Credibility Model*, the celebrity should be credible in the sense that he or she has expertise and is trustworthy. Expertise is the extent to which an endorser is perceived to be an expert with respect to the product, the problem the product solves, or the benefit a product can provide. The trustworthiness of an endorser is the degree to which the endorser is perceived to be honest and believable. According to the *Source Attractiveness Model*, attractiveness, the extent to which the celebrity is physically perceived to be attractive and is liked by the target group, plays an important role. Finally, according to the *Product Match-Up Hypothesis*, there should be an appropriate fit between the endorser's image, personality, lifestyle, and so on, and the product advertised. In this respect, it should be added that the behavior of the celebrity may turn against a brand that he or she is associated with. For instance, Tiger Woods got himself into trouble with his love life. As a result, the long-standing relationship between Woods and Accenture was ended. One specific type of endorser is influencers (discussed further on in this chapter).

The distinction between offline and online advertising is a particular one (discussed further in this and in following chapters). *Online advertising* is different from *offline advertising* in several important ways. As a response to online advertising, consumers can go all the way from building awareness to interest to desire to action, all within the same medium and within the same session. Most offline advertising formats are not suitable to accomplish this. Advertising on social media encourages (potential) customers to engage in interactions with the company or brand (*brand engagement*, the amount and intensity of user involvement), and to share brand-related knowledge with others or create their own content (*user-generated content*). Offline advertising cannot accommodate this. Online advertising is interactive in nature. Consumers click, like, and share them, or write comments. Probably the most remarkable feature of online ads is that they are increasingly personalized or customized. Social media platforms continuously collect personal data from their users, based on their online behavior. They allow advertisers to use this information to customize and personalize their messages to specific target groups, far beyond what is possible and common for advertising in traditional media (Chapter 4 goes deeper into these issues). This does not mean that the offline and online environments are separate worlds. In advertising, campaigns should reflect real life: consumers use both types of media in an integrated way. For instance, people combine online and offline shopping. There is the *ROPO* phenomenon: research online, purchase offline. Consumers consult online sources but buy in a traditional brick-and-mortar shop. Conversely, there is also the *showrooming effect*: consumers check out products in a physical shop and then buy them online. Traditional offline advertising channels, such as magazines, newspapers, and television, are still powerful media for reaching out to customers with information about new products and directing them to the web.

Contemporary advertising formats

Besides traditional forms of advertising, such as commercials on television and radio, ads in newspapers, magazines, and billboards, and banners on websites, there are several relatively new formats that have been developed more recently or have existed for a while, but have recently become popular again. Shifting media usage, advertising avoidance, skepticism toward advertising, and advertising overkill cast doubts about the effectiveness and efficiency of traditional advertising formats. Consequently, advertisers are looking for new ways to reach and persuade their audiences. This has given rise to new advertising formats. Contemporary formats have one or more of the following characteristics. First of all, nowadays, commercial messages are often *integrated* in other media content. Perhaps the most typical examples are product or brand placement and in-game advertising (see hereafter). These formats are called "*hybrid*" or "hidden but paid for" because they integrate commercial messages into editorial content in such a way that the audience is reached and influenced, often without being aware of it.

Several contemporary formats have become popular as a result of the digital revolution of the past decades. Contrary to most traditional advertising, contemporary online formats are *interactive* in that they contain a clickable link, by means of which advertisers can activate prospective customers to interact with the company or the brand. Viewers can click on the link to reach a brand or company landing page on which they can find information, leave their email address, subscribe to a newsletter, or buy products. Third, online advertising is increasingly *personalized*, or rather customized: what people see online is based on their previous online behavior. While browsing the Internet, people leave traces that reveal personal data, such as gender, age, marital status, family composition, and job, but also their lifestyles and interests. This data is analyzed by online platforms and used by advertisers to reach specific audiences with the right message at the right place, and, hopefully, at the right time.

Contemporary formats that exist online and offline are discussed first. Online formats are dealt with in the next section.

Brand placement

Brand placement, more commonly referred to as product placement, is the paid inclusion of brand identifiers in editorial content. It is a hybrid combination of advertising and sponsorship. Companies pay moviemakers, TV program producers, authors, and game developers to include brand identifiers in their editorial content. As far back as the 1930s, actors were paid by cigarette companies to smoke the brand in the movies in which they appeared. The popular television format called "soap opera" was initially conceptualized as an advertising vehicle for laundry detergents. Brand placement is big business. Worldwide, brand placement revenues show a year-on-year increase of 15% to reach more than $20 billion in 2019 and, after a standstill in the Covid-19 year 2020, it is projected that, from 2021 onwards, annual growth will be 10%–15%.[1] Products or brands were originally mainly placed in movies and TV shows, but also entire television programs can be produced to promote a brand or a company, in which case they are called *advertising-funded programs* (AFPs) (Box 2.2). In scripted programs, the brand can be integrated into the plot in a natural way and it can be shown, mentioned, or both. In non-scripted programs such as reality shows, lifestyle programs, and quizzes, brands can be used as prizes, tools, or ingredients.

Brands have also proliferated in other forms of editorial content such as music videos, books, influencer vlogs, and games. For instance, brand integration in and around games (*in-game advertising*) went from a total value of $1.4 billion in 2010 to $5.05 billion in 2020.[2] For instance, in a car game, Ford can be replaced by BMW if the player appears to be a BMW fan. Also, interactive brand placement is possible. If the viewer watches a program on a digital platform, and an actor drinks a bottle of beer, for instance by clicking on the bottle, the viewer can enter an advertising message, a promotion offer, or a Wikipedia-like environment in which comments of other users can be read and their own comments can be added. One specific form of in-game advertising is *advergames*. These are online games specifically created to promote a brand, product, service, or idea. The advertising message becomes an integral part of playing the game. Their entertainment value leads to longer interaction time and more brand immersion, and can evoke consumer responses such as forwarding the message to friends and relatives. Online games and advergames are tools that permit the online marketer to build brand awareness and brand image, drive traffic, conversion and sales, and facilitate collecting data, through a more interactive user experience. They allow voluntary self-induced exposure to brand communications and are a non-intrusive and non-interruptive means of online advertising.

Brand placement also occurs in books. For instance, Fay Weldon's *The Bulgari Connection* was commissioned by the renowned jewelry designer Bulgari; Carole Matthew's novel *The Sweetest Taboo* was sponsored by Ford; and William Boyd's short story "The Vanishing Game" was published as an interactive e-book and commissioned by Land Rover. Music videos also contain brands. For instance, Diet Coke in Lady Gaga's "Telephone," EOS lip balm in Miley Cyrus' "We can't stop," and Samsung's Galaxy Note 5 in Ariana Grande's "Focus."

Box 2.2   Practice: using online games as advertising tools

In April 2015, HBO launched the fifth season of *Game of Thrones*, an epic fantasy drama series, by organizing an online dragon hunt on Twitter. Fans of the show were able to hunt Drogon tweeting *Game of Thrones* themed GIFs as dragon bait together with the hashtag #CatchDragon. If Drogon took the bait, fans received a response to the tweet and had to retweet the post quickly before the dragon took off. Fans that retweeted quickly enough to catch him received unique content or prizes. A GIF of Drogon flying away was posted on the feed of those who weren't quick enough. The game earned more than 948.5 million tweets globally, making it the highest daily total for *Game of Thrones*. Buzz was also created on Facebook as 6.6 million people had over 12 million interactions relating to the *Game of Thrones* premiere.

Mondelez-owned Milka designed a gaming app to promote its range of biscuits in France called "the Milka biscuit saga." The brand created technology to allow multiple players to connect their iPhones simultaneously and play together. The app contained nine mini games, and players could win brand goodies and virtual cookies. Players could also create their own avatar personalizing Milka cookies. Two months after the app was released it had reached 1.1 million downloads, making it the most downloaded app in that year. The game led to a 17% increase in volume sales.

Italian fashion house Gucci partnered with an animated avatar start up Genies, to reach and engage young people. The majority of Genies' users are 18 to 25 years old and can design their custom avatars. "Gucci x Genies" made Gucci the app's exclusive provider of luxury avatar apparel, giving users access to more than 200 virtual pieces from a real-world collection. Once created, avatars could be used across messaging apps.[3]

Brand placement can be prominently or subtly integrated. Prominent integration means that the brand is very prominently present in the editorial content in that brand identifiers (products or logos) are shown frequently, are central on the screen, are shown or explicitly mentioned, and/or for a long period of time. Subtle integration means that the brand identifiers are less prominently present. Brand placement can also be more or less connected to the plot. Plot connection means that the brand is inherently part of the story or script. Less plot-connected placements have a minor role in the story. Highly plot-connected and prominent placements enhance brand awareness and memory. Highly prominent but not plot-connected placement has been shown to damage brand attitudes. The best effect on brand attitudes is reached with highly plot-connected and subtle placements. Brands can also be integrated in different ways: as props (products that are visible but not used), in-use (products that are used by the actors or characters in the show), or look-and-feel, where part of the program is "taken over" by the identity of the brands, for instance by using the brand colors or logo.

Brand placement may be an effective advertising tool. First, advertising that is integrated in editorial content cannot be avoided or "zapped." Viewers are often highly involved and connected with their favorite program; they are carried away in the program, a phenomenon called narrative transportation, telepresence, or flow. Consequently, due to meaning and affective transfer and assimilation effects, build memory and connections activate positive emotions and develop favorable attitudes toward brands used in them. Later exposure to advertising will benefit from the "mere exposure effect" (positive effect from exposure to a brief stimulus). Brand placement is most effective when there is a fit between products, characters and viewers. In brand placement, there is also an implied endorsement effect from (famous) actors. Viewers identify and build a relationship with trustworthy and likeable spokespeople, such as actors, and learn from them what a brand means and how, when, and by whom it is used (social learning). In many cases, viewers are hardly aware of the placements and do not consider them as having commercial intent. In other words, there is less "persuasion knowledge" than with advertising. Therefore, some claim that brand placement is inherently deceptive. Disclosure of brand placement may serve to increase the accessibility of the persuasive or commercial intent behind placing brands (Box 2.3).

Box 2.3   Research: program liking and brand–program fit

Integrating brands in media content can induce a process of "affect transfer" in which content-related feelings and thoughts spill over to placed brands. Additionally, it can be expected that a high degree of perceived fit between the program and the placed brand facilitates affect transfer. In other words, attitude objects (a program and a brand) that match well are strongly connected through shared associations. Furthermore, it can be expected that a high degree of perceived fit strengthens the connection between the brand and the program, making the effect of program liking on brand attitude more resistant to temporal deterioration.

These expectations were studied in a Belgian field study about the program De Designers, the local version of Project Runway. De Designers is a ten-episode advertiser-funded fashion designer competition. The program was sponsored by a well-known Belgian fashion retailer. The winner of the competition got to design his/her own clothes collection, which would be sold in the retailer's stores. The brand was an essential part of the competition and the program. Each episode contained several brand placements in the form of verbal mentions, brand logos in the designers' workshop, and so on. At regular times during the competition, the participants visited the retailer's designers or the retailer's stores. The sponsor brand was also shown and mentioned in the program's end credits. Short- and longer-term brand placement effects were measured through an online questionnaire one week and one month, respectively, after the program finale was broadcast.

The results show that program liking positively impacts brand attitude for the sponsor, both immediately after the program and in the longer run. Furthermore, the effect of program liking is reinforced by a higher degree of perceived fit between the sponsor brand and the program. A high degree of perceived brand–program fit is even more crucial in the longer term. When the perceived brand–program fit is low, the passing of time wipes out the program liking effect on brand attitude. However, this is not the case when the perceived brand–program fit is high. Advertising professionals should keep in mind that, although placing brands in well-liked content is beneficial, in the long run, a good match between the brand and the content reinforces the attitudinal benefits the brand draws from the entertaining nature of the content.

Ambient advertising

Ambient advertising is "advertising with a 'wow' factor." It is usually original, surprising, and spectacular, and mostly associated with outdoor advertising. Examples are light projections on famous landmarks, huge posters on building sites, transformation of public vehicles, street art, or "flash mobs," sudden and temporary pop-up events to promote a brand. Related terms for this type of advertising are street marketing and guerrilla marketing.

Stealth advertising

Stealth advertising is the use of marketing practices that do not disclose or reveal the true relationship between the message and the company that pays for it. It is an advertising method in which consumers are often not aware that they are being exposed to advertising. For instance, a mobile phone manufacturer paid students to walk around in busy places and ask people to take their picture "with their brand new mobile phone with the fantastic camera." Obviously, since the company's commercial intent is not disclosed, stealth advertising is often considered to be an unethical practice.

Buzz marketing

Word of mouth has always been important in influencing people's buying behavior. *Buzz marketing* is advertising that uses public relations techniques. It is deliberately creating news, giving people a reason to talk about products and brands, and making it easier for conversations to take place. Buzz marketing is aimed at spreading the message through the personal network of consumers. It is "organized word of mouth." Typically, people like to talk about intimacies, sex, the extraordinary, the unusual, fun things, a story with a special angle, and secrets.

Content marketing and storytelling

Content marketing is a strategic marketing approach focused on creating and distributing valuable, relevant, and consistent content to attract and retain a clearly defined audience and, ultimately, to drive profitable customer action. Content marketing usually does not have a direct product selling intent. It is creating and communicating content that is relevant for the target audience and, in that way, builds up knowledge, trust, and a favorable disposition toward brands. In traditional media, for instance, *sponsored magazines* are magazines that are produced by marketers ("owned media") to create context for and promote their brands. They look and feel like ordinary magazines, offer content that relates to the products of the company, and integrate the company's brands in a subtle way. An online example is native advertising (see hereafter).

A special form of content marketing is *storytelling*. Advertisers increasingly use storytelling to create a meaningful context for their brands. Stories create context for a message, and they are appealing and easily remembered. Stories can help customers to identify with a brand, its history, the founder of the brand, brand myths, brand heroes, the characters in the story, the lifestyle a brand represents, and so on, and they are easily shared with other people. Companies that do storytelling advertising well are Lego and Harley-Davidson (Box 2.4).

Box 2.4   Practice: Guinness: made of more

For many years, the beer brand Guinness focused on dramatizing product truths with the tagline "Good things come to those who wait." However, half the population of the world who drink Guinness don't actually have to wait for it to be poured on tap, because they buy it in bottles or cans. Guinness decided to develop a new message strategy and a new positioning approach, focusing on the shared attitude between brand, product, and drinker. The new strategy was based on the idea that Guinness is a bold brand and a bold product for bold people. Guinness identified an aspirational and bold consumer attitude amongst its beer drinkers. They are those in life who don't just want to follow the crowd, but instead make bold choices and carve their own path. In 2012, the message strategy was changed accordingly, with a new tagline "Made of More." Guinness tells stories of how unexpected character in people and beer enriches the world around us, and told stories about contemporary, often controversial, themes including disability, war, gang violence, LGBT rights, and racial equality. The Made of More stories were distributed on various social media channels.

Guinness made campaign videos about a group of friends playing wheelchair basketball. At the end of the game, all the friends unexpectedly stand and walk away from their wheelchairs, revealing that only one of the players is wheelchair bound. In "The Sapeurs" a real group of men form "The Society of the Elegant Persons of the Congo." Ordinary people by day, by night they dress in flamboyant suits, coming together to bring joy to their community. The next major project in 2015, the year of the Rugby World Cup, was to create videos to uncover two rugby stories that went beyond rugby physicality that challenged conventional views of men and masculinity. The first one was the story of rugby's first openly gay player (Gareth Thomas) who kept his sexuality secret for years. He found the courage to confront his demons and "come out," with the encouragement of his teammates. The second was the story of Springbok Ashwin Willemse, who had to choose between two paths: a notorious Cape Town gang and rugby. The Guinness story celebrates his choice to defy his circumstances. In 2017, Guinness told the story of John Hammond, a man with a passion for music of black origin. He stood up to prejudice in the 1930s, championing the potential of black and white artists working together. The story demonstrates Guinness' belief in character, integrity, and communion. In 2018, the Compton Cowboys video was released: young men whose passion is to ride horses in South Central LA, a region better known for its crime and violence. By refusing to be defined by our environment and rising above it we can inspire those around us to do the same. The story was launched with a range of formats and on multiple social media platforms. It has become a best-practice case study used by both Google and Facebook. In 2019, *Liberty Fields* told the story of Japan's first women's rugby team, celebrating the athletes' resilience and strength in the face of social prejudice. The film was backed by a documentary, social media activations, an ITV (UK) special, and venue takeovers.

The Made of More work received 148 creative awards, including gold at the 2020 IPA Effectiveness Awards. The campaign videos received many millions of views on social media. Follow-up stories behind the Compton Cowboys held viewers' attention for minutes. Brand awareness increased significantly and, in consumer research, Guinness scored significantly higher than the category average on several important brand values. The brand realized significantly higher volumes than before, and return on investment was higher than ever and also greater than their competitors. Thanks to the "consistency x creativity effect," Made of More is estimated to have generated an extra £1bn in sales for Guinness in Ireland and Great Britain alone.[4]

The formats discussed so far can be developed online and offline. The next section examines online formats.

Online advertising formats

Brand websites

Brand websites are sites with specific brand-related information and/or services. Although, strictly speaking, they are not advertising, they play an important role in the advertising context. A brand website is necessary for "maintenance communication" all year round, 24 hours a day. Additionally, it is not just the brand website that is a communication tool, but also its social media presence, such as a Facebook brand page or an Instagram brand profile. A tailor-made brand site can also be used for a short period during an advertising campaign. These temporary sites are also called *micro-sites*. They often function as "landing pages" for online advertising campaigns. Online advertising can drive an audience directly to a specific URL, so that the pertinent information is only a few clicks away. They are a good way to isolate a user and keep them focused on one product or a specific range of products, or to convert a visitor who has clicked on a link in an online ad into a "lead," and further activate him or her to become a customer.

Unlike traditional advertising, which are push instruments, online marketing communications often require an action from the consumer as the Internet is a pull medium. Websites need continuous traffic-generating efforts (to attract visitors to the site). Successful traffic generators are online advertising, including the URL on corporate media (stationery such as business cards, letterheads, and brochures), on packaging, and in offline advertising. An important technique to generate traffic to a website is *Search Engine Optimization* (SEO). Search engines have been called "the new homepage for brands and businesses." It is thus important to be high on the list in search engines. Some web agencies are specialists in registering sites in top and niche search engines and in improving their rankings on the engine. Another way of increasing search engine share-of-voice is *keyword buying*, one of the online advertising techniques explained below. Presence on social media can generate free *organic reach* (*earned media*): followers of these brand pages or profiles and fans like, share, and comment upon branded posts on these platforms.

Native advertising

In traditional media, there are advertorials and infomercials. *Advertorials* are print advertisements (in newspapers and magazines) that match the form and style of the medium. Infomercials are a similar format, but on television. They look and feel like a genuine short TV program, but in fact are long TV spots. Both formats are to a certain extent "hidden." Advertisers and media are obliged to disclose the commercial nature of this editorial content, but readers or viewers often overlook this disclosure and see the message as (partly) editorial. *Native advertising* refers to a similar online advertising format. Examples are the advertisements that appear in the Facebook newsfeed or in online newspapers. The word "native" refers to the content's coherence with other content on the website. In native advertising, ads can be shown naturally and without interrupting the flow of, for instance, browsing through a Facebook newsfeed or online news media. Often, native ads are content marketing pieces that often also contain a call-to-action, a link that redirects readers to a landing page.

In-app advertisements

In-app advertisements are displayed within a mobile app. These can be anything from a sponsored post or tweet to a banner or autoplay video in a game. They can be static or contain animations integrated into the app. Native ads in apps are a more advanced version of banner or video ads in that they are even more integrated into the app, making them less intrusive. Features such as location data and advanced campaign analytics make in-app ads a highly targeted path to reaching and converting users.

Influencer marketing

An *influencer* is an individual who has the power to affect purchase decisions of others because of their authority, knowledge, position, or relationship with the audience. Most of the time they have built a reputation for their knowledge and expertise on one or more topics. They are active in social media, where they have accounts on social media platforms. They regularly post about these topics and thereby generate and actively engage with enthusiastic, engaged followers who pay close attention to their posts. Influencers differ from celebrities who endorse brands in advertising in that influencers are not "famous" because of sports performance, singing, or acting in movies. They usually have become well-known and highly regarded by their followers because of the credibility and trustworthiness they have built up as an opinion leader. Mega-influencers are social superstars with more than one million followers; they are often celebrities. Macro-influencers have between 100,000 and one million followers. Micro-influencers have between 1,000 and 100,000 followers and, while their following may be small(ish), their authenticity is high. Finally, nano-influencers have fewer than 1,000 followers, but can have a big influence with a comparatively narrow niche.

Marketers use social media influencers because they can create trends and encourage their followers to buy products they promote. Ninety percent of marketers believe that influencer marketing is effective, and indeed they may be right: 70% of teenage YouTube subscribers say they relate to YouTube creators more than traditional celebrities, 91% of millennials trust online reviews as much as friends and family, and nearly 40% of Twitter users say they've made a purchase as a direct result of a tweet from an influencer. Brands can ask influencers to give exposure to their products in return for compensation in cash or kind (products). It is estimated that every $1 spent on influencer marketing generates $5.20 extra revenue. Micro-influencers appear to be more effective than macro-influencers. Influencer marketing is booming business. In 2021, influencer marketing budgets are estimated to be $13.8 billion. In a survey, 17% of marketers claim to have a budget for content marketing, and 75% of them have a dedicated budget for influencer marketing. Sixty-seven percent use

Instagram (down from 80% in 2020), 45% TikTok (increasing sharply), 43% Facebook, and 36% YouTube.[5]

Location-based advertising

Location-based advertising targets advertising messages to consumers based on their location to promote location-based services. Examples of location-based services are personal navigation (how do I get there?), point-of-interest (what's that?), reviews (what is the best restaurant in the neighborhood?), friend-finder (where are you?), and family-tracker services (where is my child?). These services are an opportunity for marketers who can target consumers with messages at the right moment and the right location to improve local shopping and buying experiences. *Geo-targeting* is the practice of delivering user content to someone based on their geographic location. It can be done on the city or postal code level, by using an IP address or device ID, or with GPS signals.

Affiliate marketing

Affiliate marketing or affiliate networking is a performance-based marketing technique often used by online retailers that reward one or more affiliates for each visitor brought about by the affiliate's own marketing efforts (Figure 2.1). There are several options for affiliate compensation: commission (for every sale which is a direct result of click-through traffic from the affiliate's website), pay per click, pay per lead (for every person who signs up for something), residual income (for every time a customer renews a service or purchases additional products after initial click-through from an affiliate's website), or pay per sale (for every time a person purchases a product or service after clicking through an affiliate's website).

Nowadays, online advertising is mainly *programmatic advertising,* an automated, technology-driven method of buying, selling, or fulfilling ad placements. It uses real-time systems, algorithms, and rules to deliver the automated purchase of data-driven, targeted, and relevant online display, video, or mobile ads. In the following sections we describe specific formats in programmatic advertising.

Figure 2.1   Affiliate marketing

Search Engine Advertising (SEA): Google AdWords

Google's search engine business model is largely based on *Google AdWords* (also called *keyword buying* or *Search Engine Advertising* (SEA)). This is a marketplace where companies pay to have their website displayed at the top of a search results page, based on the keywords of Google users. SEA allows precise targeting of an interested audience. When people go to Google, they are looking for something specific and they are literally telling Google what they are interested in by typing out words around products and services (Figure 2.2). SEA is performance-based and its cost depends on the effectiveness of the campaign. If the ad does not result in clicks, leads or sales, companies don't pay. In the *Display Network* option, ads also show up on other websites and blogs Google has an affiliation with. It is estimated that, in 2021 in the U.S.A., SEA accounts for 44% of all online advertising spending, or $56 billion of the $130 billion in digital ad spend.[6]

The video sharing platform YouTube is owned by Google, and follows the same logic of keyword buying. YouTube offers a variety of ad formats. *Display* ads appear to the right of the feature video, above the video suggestions list – on desktop only. *Overlay* ads are semi-transparent ads that appear on the lower 20% of a video – on desktop only. *Skippable video* ads are the ads shown before, during, or after a video which a viewer

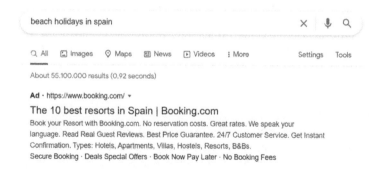

Figure 2.2   An ad on Google

can skip after a few seconds. *Non-skippable video* ads are video ads that viewers must watch before they can view the main video. *Bumper* ads must be watched for up to six seconds before the main video starts to roll. *Sponsored cards* provide content relevant to the video, for example, products featured in the main video. Advertisers pay for an in-stream ad when somebody watches at least 30 seconds of the ad (unless it is shorter). They pay for a video discovery ad when somebody clicks on the ad.

Advertising on social networking sites and blogs

Advertising through social networking sites can be very effective to target both new and returning customers, test ads in real time, use platform analytics to determine best performing ads, and grow a brand's fan base and sales. Additionally, there is virtually no limit to a company's ability to scale the size of a campaign. In what follows, examples are given of ad formats on a number of social media platforms. Each platform has an ad manager module in which these formats can be selected and a campaign can be developed.

Facebook offers four advertising possibilities: inside the newsfeed on desktop or mobile, right-hand sidebar on desktop, and audience networking. Advertising inside the newsfeed is also called native advertising. With audience networking advertising (making the advertising campaign not only visible on Facebook (and on Instagram, which is owned by Facebook), but also on affiliated websites, companies can expand their campaigns to thousands of other websites and apps. Instagram offers the same format, except for the right-hand sidebar option. By means of native advertising, Facebook and Instagram want to integrate their ads into the natural flow of the experience as seamlessly as possible. Ads on Facebook usually have a "call to action" (CTA), such as: Book now, Contact us, Use app, Play game, Shop now, Sign up, and Watch video.

Twitter offers advertising formats in four categories. *Promoted tweets* can contain text, images, GIFs, polls, or accounts. *Promoted videos* can be pre-roll, videos in which sponsorship is amplified, first-view videos that only remain available for 24 hours, and are aimed at creating mass awareness, and promoted live videos. *Brand ads* can be branded emojis, brand reminders, promoted moments, or promoted trends. Finally, *cards* can be website cards, app cards, carousels, and conversation cards. The latter have an embedded CTA.

Pinterest provides four advertising formats. *Standard pins* appear in the newsfeed like regular pins, but they contain the word "Promoted." They allow companies to showcase products and content in image or video formats. When the Pinterest user clicks a standard pin, they are led directly to a landing page of the brand. *Carousel ads* are similar to standard pins, except that they allow users to swipe through two to five images or videos (named "cards"). Each card can contain its own link leading to up to five different landing pages. With *Shopping pins*, a company can upload products from its catalogue and turn them into pins. Brands use them to promote things such as the latest spring fashion, living room decor, fitness equipment, and more. The campaign objective for shopping pins is conversions, i.e., driving sales. Finally, *Promoted App pins* make it easy for people to discover and download apps directly from Pinterest. When someone clicks on a Promoted App pin, they can download their new app without having to leave Pinterest.

LinkedIn offers four ad formats. *Sponsored Content* is native ads that appear directly in the LinkedIn feed of professions a company wants to reach, and comes in three different formats: single image ads, video ads, and carousel ads. With *Message Ads*, companies can reach their prospects on LinkedIn Messaging. With Message Ads, companies can send direct messages to their prospects to spark immediate action. A *Dynamic Ad* enables a company to personalize their creative approach for each member in their target audience. Dynamic Ads use LinkedIn profile data

– like photo, company name, and job title – to personalize ads. Finally, *Text Ads* are simple pay-per-click (PPC) or cost per 1,000 impressions (CPM) ads. Companies only pay for the ads that work, per click, or per impression.

Snapchat also provides a number of ad formats. *Top Snap Only* ads display a single piece of content at the top of the feed. These ads are suitable for promoting events, sales, or other one-off activities. Brands often use them to drive people to a website landing page, to watch a long-form video, or to install an app. *Long-Form Video* ads can be up to 10 minutes long. *Web View* ads are like Top Snap Only ads, with the additional feature that lets users swipe up on the ad and go to a particular URL. These ads are particularly useful for introducing a brand. When users click an *App Install* ad, they are taken straight to the relevant page at the appropriate download store to download the app that's being promoted. *Sponsored Lenses* allow Snapchatters to make fun modifications to their selfies and other images. A *Sponsored geofilter* is a graphic overlay that Snapchatters can place on their snaps. Advertisers can create geofilters, based on where they are physically located.

Finally, on TikTok, the *Video Creation Kit* helps advertisers to design their ads. This kit provides video and image templates that advertisers can customize using their own existing images. It also comes with hundreds of options for free background music. TikTok currently offers three ad types. A *brand takeover ad* will appear instantly when a user opens TikTok. The ad can then be redirected to an internal or external link – either another video on TikTok or an external website or app. *In-feed ads* are native ads placed either at the bottom of organic TikTok videos or in the feed as part of the video queue type of product. These ads also redirect to a website or an app. Advertisers can also partner with TikTok's marketing team to create a *sponsored hashtag challenge* that encourages users to share content on TikTok on the brand's behalf.

Viral marketing

Companies and brands rely on three types of approaches to reach their audiences. First of all, they use *owned media*, tools the content of which they develop and distribute themselves, such as newsletters, sponsored magazines, websites, Facebook pages, or other social media profiles. Second, they launch advertising campaigns – this is *paid media*. Finally, they use viral marketing to generate what is called *earned media* or *organic reach*: consumers react to owned or paid media by liking, sharing, and commenting on branded online materials, and in that way "spread the word" for free. Part of this earned media is *user-generated content* (UGC). Formally, UGC is non-organizational media activity on third-party sites, for example posts on social media, comments in community forums, online ratings and reviews, feedback on blogs, and reaction on podcasts or videos. UGC is manifested in numerous formats: text, hyperlinks to other content, moving or fixed images, audio, music, animation, video or a mix of these elements. The essence of UGC is that it is personal, published and outside the domain of the contributor, and consequently it often costs nothing to create; users' actions in social media are shared with their networks, as well as across the brand pages, widening the potential audience; other consumers identify blog articles created by other users as more credible; search engine results are often based on UGC; UGC can assist the consumer decision journey; and UGC can transform elements of a business. On the other hand, the content is outside the organization's control, it is without guarantees and can be unpredictable, creating risk as the organization may be promoted negatively as well as positively.

Some researchers talk about a transition from a bowling model to a *pinball model*. Before consumers had access to new media that allows them to largely disseminate their own views on products and brands, marketers' activity resembled playing bowling: they would use mass media (alley) and throw a ball (message) toward pins (consumers), hoping to touch as many as possible. Nowadays, this interaction is more like a pinball game: marketers drop a ball (message) in the pinball machine (new media), and try to keep it in the game as long as possible by operating the flippers (consumers). However, like the ball in a pinball machine, this message can be thrown back and forth by bumpers, kickers, and slingshots (or consumers portraying their own views on the product or brand), changing the direction of the message constantly. This "pinball game" shows that the new marketplace rewards participatory, sincere, and less directive marketing styles, which reinforces the importance of understanding and managing earned media.

Viral marketing is a set of techniques used to keep the ball in the game, i.e., stimulate organic reach and UGC, in other words to stimulate brand engagement or eWOM (*electronic word-of-mouth*). Viral marketing attempts to stimulate the strongest of all consumer triggers, namely personal recommendation. The goal of viral marketing is to inspire individuals to share a message to friends, family, and other individuals to create exponential growth in the number of its recipients. Viral marketing campaigns work best in groups with strong common interests, because they allow marketers to spread selective messages to selective groups. Different methods of obtaining UGC have been employed, such as directly petitioning customers. For instance, TripAdvisor has a program designed to obtain content from guests to generate additional postings. Other methods of gaining UGC are via CTA, inviting users to collaborate, compete, or celebrate. The call to collaborate asks for content to be shared by posing questions, the answers to which could result in prizes being awarded. The call to compete centers around an integrated competition with a prerequisite for a purchase to be made; the call to celebrate harnesses friendship around a larger event.

Creativity in advertising

The most general way to define creativity is "a violation of expectations." Creativity in advertising has two dimensions. Creative ads are "different," highly unique, and novel. Ads can be original in that they contain elements that are surprising or different from the obvious or in that they combine different ideas or switch from one perspective to the other. They can contain unexpected details or become more complicated or sophisticated, or combine previously unrelated ideas. The impact of creative advertising is generally assumed to be in its attention-grabbing potential. This is assumed to lead to more and deeper processing of the ad's content, and higher recognition and recall of the brand and message elements. Moreover, creative ads increase the willingness of viewers to view the ad again. Creativity thus stimulates a higher frequency of exposure and repeat message processing.

At the same time, to stand out and persuade, creative ads should also be functional, i.e., relevant and meaningful for the target audiences, be in line with the campaign objectives, and a translation of the campaign message strategy. Creativity in advertising should thus support the message strategy and be appealing to customers not only because the ad is surprising and novel, but also because it is relevant to them. Pure artistic creativity, without the necessary strategic focus, runs the risk of being noticed and liked, but may also cause distraction from the core message. The audience may remember the ad, but at the same time may remain completely in the dark about which brand was talking to them and what it wanted to say. Non-strategic creativity may indeed lead to brand confusion and lack of message processing. Advertising is an expensive tool to support the marketing of products and services; if it fails to do that, it is bad advertising, no matter how creative it is.

Notes

1. https://www.pqmedia.com/product/global-product-placement-forecast-2020/.
2. https://statista.com/statistics/238140/global-video-games-advertising-revenue.
3. https://www.contagious.com/io/article/genies-in-gucci.
4. https://www.thinkbox.tv/case-studies/brand-films/guinness/; https://www.marketingweek.com/facebook-instagram-guinness/; https://www.warc.com/newsandopinion/opinion/how-guinness-consistency-x-creativity-formula-earned-it-an-ipa-gold/3870.
5. https://influencermarketinghub.com/influencer-marketing-statistics/.
6. K.C. Laudon and C.G. Traver (2019), *E-commerce 2018: Business, Technology, Society*. Pearson.

3 How advertising works

Often it is hard to predict how a consumer will respond to advertising or how someone will process an advertising message. Many factors have an impact on how advertising works: consumer goals, product type, the situation the consumer is in (hurried or distracted by others, for example), involvement in the product category, and social, psychological or cultural factors. Moreover, the digital revolution has changed advertising fundamentally, in that consumers have partly taken over brand communications and interact with each other on an unprecedented massive scale. No single theory can explain it all. Some models are applicable in some situations for some kinds of people and for some categories of products. This chapter should therefore be seen as a set of theories that are all relevant, but in different situations, for different products, and for different kinds of consumers.

Hierarchy-of-effects models

According to *hierarchy-of-effects* (HoE) *models,* consumers sequentially go through different stages in responding to advertising, namely a cognitive, an affective, and a behavioral stage, or a think–feel–do sequence. A hierarchy-of-effects model assumes that things have to happen in a certain order, implying that the earlier effects form necessary conditions in order for the later effects to occur. During the cognitive stage, consumers engage in thinking processes which lead to awareness and knowledge of the advertised brand. In the affective stage, emotional or evaluative responses occur and attitudes toward the brand are formed. The behavioral stage refers to undertaking actions with respect to the advertised brand, such as visiting a store or a website, or buying a product. In traditional HoE models, consumers should first learn or become aware of a brand. Afterwards, they develop affective responses and form an attitude towards it. Finally, this feeling or attitude makes the consumers want to buy the brand. The task of advertising is to lead the consumers through these successive stages for a positive end result (sales). The oldest HoE model is the *AIDA Model*. It stands for: Attention (cognitive), Interest, Desire (affective), Action (behavior). It was originally designed to train salespeople to go through these four stages, in that order, to close the sale. The *Lavidge and Steiner Model* proposes the goals of the different stages in an advertising campaign: Brand awareness, Brand knowledge (cognitive), Brand Liking, Preference, Conviction (affective), Purchase (behavior). A similar approach is proposed by the *DAGMAR Model* (Defining Advertising Goals for Measuring Advertising Results), which will be discussed in Chapter 4. Another example is the Adoption–Diffusion Model, also called the *AIETA Model*. This model proposes the five stages of the consumers' adoption process of innovations: Awareness (cognitive), Interest, Evaluation (affective), Trial, Adoption (behavior). Traditional hierarchy-of-effects models are still an inspiration for advertising campaigns today.

However, a lot of disagreement exists regarding the sequence of the different stages, and several alternative models have been developed. An example is the *low-involvement hierarchy-of-effects model*, according to which consumers, after frequent exposure to marketing messages, might buy the product and decide afterwards how they feel about it (cognitive–behavioral–affective hierarchy). Another framework is the *experiential hierarchy-of-effects model* in which consumers' affective responses toward a product lead them to buy it and, if necessary, they reflect on it later. This would suggest an affective–behavioral–cognitive sequence.

An integration of the different HoE models is the *Foote–Cone–Belding* (FCB) grid. In the original FCB grid philosophy, four different product categories are distinguished, based on two dimensions, i.e., the high–low involvement and think–feel. *Involvement* is the importance people attach to a product or a buying decision, the extent to which one has to think it over and the level of perceived risk associated with an inadequate brand choice. Products such as cars, education, and jewelry are for most consumers high involvement products, while most people consider cookies, ice cream, and laundry detergents as low involvement ones. The *think–feel dimension* represents a continuum reflecting the extent to which a decision is made on a cognitive or an affective basis. For certain products, such as sugar, mineral water, paper towels, soap, and banks, cognitive elements are important, while for products such as cakes, ice cream, and perfume, affective elements seem to have more impact on the buying decision process.

Figure 3.1 shows the different sequences in each of the four situations. Purchase decisions in the first quadrant are characterized by high involvement and rational decision criteria. Here, the consumer first wants to learn about the product, then could develop a positive attitude toward it, and finally may buy it. This could be the case for deciding on an insurance policy or for buying a new computer or major household appliance. In this quadrant, the classical hierarchy of effects would hold. The main advertising strategy for such products can be summarized as "selling is telling": the consumer needs a lot of factual, rational information and arguments to be persuaded. The second quadrant concerns high involvement products for which the consumer seeks important emotional or lifestyle arguments to buy them. In this case, the consumer first wants to be emotionally attracted by the brand image, then he or she collects information, and finally buys the product. Jewelry, perfume, fashion, and holidays may be examples that fit in this category. The appropriate strategy here is to create an appealing and emotional lifestyle universe. In the third quadrant, product decisions are located that require a minimum of cognitive effort and tend to become routinized because of habit formation. The assumed sequence is first buying the product, then learning more about it, and finally developing an attitude after product or brand usage. Toilet paper, sugar, paper tissues, and detergents are examples that would fit in this quadrant. The advertising approach called for here is "rational conditioning," i.e., establishing a link between the brand name and one or a couple of unique factional and rational arguments. The fourth quadrant reflects decision-making regarding products which can be termed "life's little pleasures." The assumed sequence here is: buy the product, experience an affective response, and learn to know the product afterwards. Examples that fit this category might be soft drinks, ice cream, and chocolate bars. The appropriate advertising here is "affective conditioning," i.e., establish a link between the brand and a good feeling.

The *Rossiter–Percy* grid is a modification of the FCB grid which again classifies buying decisions in four categories, based on the dimensions of high–low involvement and fulfilling a transformational or informational buying motive. *Transformational buying motives* consist of positive motivations, such as sensory gratification, social approval, or intellectual

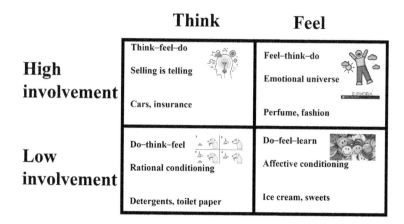

Figure 3.1   The FCB grid

stimulation, while *informational buying motives* refer to reducing or reversing negative motivations such as solving or avoiding a problem. Examples of products for which transformational motives prevail are ice cream, cosmetics, and perfume. Examples of informational products are detergents, babies' diapers, and insurance products.

The interesting insight of the FCB grid is that the HoE that consumers go through may be different depending on the buying context. However, the misconception of the original framework is that involvement (low or high) and buying motivations (think or feel) are not characteristics of product types but of people in a buying situation. For instance, cars can be in each of the four quadrants. One person who wants to buy a car may need a lot of factual product information, in which case this consumer would be in quadrant 1. Other consumers may buy cars that correspond with their (aspired) lifestyle, in which case they do not need so much information; rather, they are triggered by emotions a car evokes and the extent to which they feel the car is a representation or extension of their lifestyle; they are in quadrant 2. Still other people may just go for the cheapest car in the category, which make them quadrant 3 consumers. Finally, some consumers may look for a car that looks nice and has a cool color; that would put them in quadrant 4. Additionally, for most consumers, buying a car for the first time is a high-involvement decision while, at a later age, they may become less involved because buying a car is a less risky financial decision for them. Indeed, many products are highly involving the first time you buy them, but become less so when you have already bought the product frequently, because of habit formation. Consider insurance: the first time a person buys a new insurance (for instance, when buying a house or an apartment), this is probably a relatively highly involving decision. However, when a year later this person is invited to pay the insurance fee, she will probably only spend a couple of minutes to pay the fee online. The insurance has become a low involvement product. Whether or not a product is highly or lowly involving thus depends on the buying situation, and also on the buying context. Take food: in "normal" circumstances, a person may be very health conscious, and buy food on the basis of its ingredients, how it was produced, and so on. This person is in quadrant 1. However, this same person may be all into buying an indulgent McDonald's hamburger with fries on the side when he or she returns home from a party at night and is very hungry. For a while, this same person is in quadrant 4 – the same person and the same product category, but a different buying situation. A wine-loving individual who routinely drinks wine every day may usually buy relatively cheap wine he or she is used to and likes. He is a quadrant 4 person. However, if he buys wine because he has invited good friends for dinner, he may study the label or the type of wine, or its reputation before making a choice. He is temporarily a quadrant 1 or maybe a quadrant 2 person. Thus, the FCB is not so much a categorization of product types, but rather a categorization of a person in a buying situation with respect to a specific product. For companies, it is thus a segmentation and positioning tool rather than a rigid product categorization. For instance, if you sell sports cars, BMWs, and Alfa Romeos, you will probably have to target consumers who are quadrant 2 buyers. If you sell hamburgers and fries, you will have to target quadrant 4 people who – structurally or occasionally – want to give themselves a treat.

The advantage of HoE models is that they provide a framework for advertising objectives and campaign effectiveness measurement (see Chapters 4 and 5). A major critique of HoE models is that empirical support for the fact that consumers go through each of a series of stages every time is lacking. Therefore, to base advertising strictly on HoE models may not always be the most effective or relevant strategy.

Attitude formation and change

An *attitude* is a person's overall evaluation of, for example, an object, a product, a person, an organization, or an ad. In this view, an attitude toward a particular brand can be considered as a measure of how much a person likes or dislikes the brand, or of the extent to which he or she holds a favorable view of it. The relevance of brand attitudes is the assumption that the more favorable brand attitudes are, the more likely a purchase of the brand becomes. So, an important challenge for advertising is to change attitudes in favor of the company's brand. Attitudes play an important role in HoE models too, but in these models they are primarily defined as affective reactions in a hierarchical setting. However, that does not need to be the case. An attitude can be assumed to consist of three components. The cognitive component reflects knowledge and beliefs about the brand; the affective component represents the feelings associated with the brand; and the behavioral component refers to action readiness (behavioral intentions) with respect to the object. You may love Timberland shoes (affective component) because you know they are durable and convenient to wear (cognitive component) and that is why you intend to buy them (behavioral component). To change attitudes, marketers might concentrate on changing one or more of these three components. Tom Ford might stress the fact that its clothes are neat, cool, and stylish, thereby trying to influence the feelings associated with it by image-building. Advertising campaigns trying to influence the consumer on an affective basis often use emotional ads containing no or very few product arguments. Miele might address the quality and durability of its appliances to change consumers' beliefs. Advertising will probably use many strong arguments to illustrate the numerous benefits of Miele. Coca-Cola might run a promotion campaign in which consumers can receive a fabulous Coke mobile phone in return for a certain amount of cola caps, to induce consumers to buy (a lot of) the brand. Many marketers and advertisers consider developing solid and well-positioned brands as their prime mission.

Several advertising models have been developed that are all relevant and able to explain how advertising persuades consumers, but each for particular situations. These different advertising models regarding attitude formation and change can be classified along two dimensions. The first refers to the way attitudes are formed – primarily cognitive, affective, or behavioral; the second is about how the message is processed. With respect to the latter, several *dual-process theories* have been developed. What most of these theories have in common is that they distinguish between information processing that is unconscious, rapid, automatic, and does not require much cognitive capacity, and information processing that is conscious, slow, deliberative, and requires availability of cognitive resources. The *Elaboration Likelihood Model* (ELM) is one that has been used extensively to predict and explain consumer attitudinal responses to advertising, and distinguishes between central and peripheral processing, depending on how optimal processing conditions are. Processing conditions are determined by *Motivation, Ability and Opportunity* (MAO) to process (elaborate on) a message.

Motivation is the willingness to engage in behavior, make decisions, pay attention, and process information. Motivation is to a large extent influenced by consumer needs and goals. Consumer needs can be functional, symbolic, or hedonic. *Functional needs* pertain to solving consumer problems. Consumers buy detergents to clean dirty clothes and hire a baby-sitter because they cannot leave their baby unattended. *Symbolic needs* relate to how we see ourselves and how we would like to be perceived by others. Youngsters may wear Calvin Klein jeans to show they are trendy. *Hedonic needs* reflect consumers' desires for sensory pleasure. People buy chocolates, wine, or cool clothes to indulge themselves, and for sensory gratification. Needs/goals can also be classified as *approach or promotion goals*, and *avoidance or prevention goals*. The former pertain to positive outcomes while the latter relate to avoiding negative outcomes. For example, consumers can decide to shop at a certain supermarket because it offers them a nice shopping experience (= approach, promotion) or because they do not have to drive far (= avoidance, prevention). A consumer who plans to buy a new car is probably motivated to process advertising on cars. However, the needs that this particular consumer is pursuing have an important impact on information processing and the benefits he or she is receptive to. If the consumer is mainly driven by functional needs, he or she may want clear information on price, safety, fuel consumption, and so on, while a status appeal or an ad showing driving sensations may be more effective when symbolic or hedonic needs prevail. The same goes for approach/promotion goals and avoidance/prevention goals: when the former are prevalent then advertising should bring a message focused on positive outcomes (you feel the excitement when driving this car), while for the latter goals a message should emphasize negative outcomes (the excellent air bags will protect you during a crash).

So, in order to be persuasive, advertising should tap into consumers' motivational concepts and advertisers need to understand what goals consumers are trying to accomplish by buying the product. Additionally, consumers will be more motivated by messages that relate to what is highly involving for them. This involvement can be structural or situational (temporarily). For instance, if a consumer is structurally highly involved in food, he will be motivated to process food ads most of the time. If this is not the case, he may be temporarily more highly involved in food when he is having his best friend over for dinner. Similarly, a consumer may be a car freak, and therefore be very motivated to process any message about cars. Conversely, she may be only motivated to process car ads when she plans to buy a new car.

Although someone is motivated to do something, he or she may be unable to do it. *Ability* refers to the resources needed to achieve a particular goal. One may be motivated to process a computer ad, but when it is full of technical details one may not be able to process and understand it because of a lack of technical knowledge. Advertisements that show a context that is far away from a consumer's daily lifestyle may be hard to relate to, and hence more difficult to understand. A person may be motivated to buy a particular house, but after learning what it is going to cost after renovation, stamp duty, land registration fees, and so on, might be unable to buy it because of insufficient money. Finally, *opportunity* deals with the extent to which the situation enables a person to obtain her goals. A consumer may be motivated to buy Ice Tea Peach, but if the supermarket runs out of it, the consumer does not have the opportunity to buy it. A consumer may be motivated to process the information of a particular ad, but if the phone rings, she does not have the opportunity to pay attention to it. A consumer who is waiting at a red traffic light may start to process an outdoor ad, but when the light turns green, the opportunity to process the ad disappears. Also, when the ad contains little or no information, it does not provide the opportunity to elaborate on it.

The ELM and the effects of the MAO factors on advertising processing and attitude formation are presented in Figure 3.2. If motivation, ability and opportunity are all high, the elaboration likelihood is said to be high and consumers are expected to engage in *central-route processing* (Box 3.1). This means that they are willing to elaborate on the information and evaluate the arguments. Depending on the quality and credibility of the arguments, consumers will react by producing counter-, support, or neutral arguments, which induce a negative, positive, or no attitude change, respectively. For example, when thinking of McDonald's, consumers might think of how good McDonald's burgers and fries taste: a support argument. On the other hand, consumers might also think of how unhealthy fast food is: a counter-argument. Furthermore, consumers might just think of the red and yellow colors of a McDonald's restaurant: a neutral argument. Attitudes formed via the central route are long-lasting and profound, and prove to be good predictors of later behavior and are fairly resistant to other persuasive messages. On the other hand, if one or more of the MAO factors is/are low, consumers are more likely to process the information peripherally. The result of *peripheral-route processing* is not real information processing, but an evaluation based on simple, peripheral cues, such as background music, humor, an attractive model or endorser in the ad, the number of arguments used, and so on. In other words, a favorable attitude toward the Nespresso brand might be formed because the consumer likes George Clooney, because the consumer is fond of the polar bears in a Coca-Cola commercial, because she assumed that the high price of a car model is a sign of superior quality, or that French wine is invariably good. However, such attitudes do not necessarily last long and do not go very deep. Consumers often pay attention to peripheral cues because in many ads peripheral cues form the only processable information under circumstances of low motivation, limited ability or limited opportunity. Ads without attractive peripheral cues, but with an easy-to-process, product-related message, might also work under low MAO, simply because not many resources are required to understand the message and/or the cognitive resources to form counter-arguments are lacking.

The above might suggest that the central route pertains to cognitive attitude formation (people think carefully about the substance of the message), while peripheral-route processing is more likely to give rise to affective attitude formation (people rely on how the ad makes them feel instead of what the ad really tells them). However, in reality, it is more complicated. The ELM, as well as other dual-processing models, assumes that, under different MAO conditions, both rational arguments and affect may give rise to peripheral and central processing. For instance, research shows that when individuals focus on ideals (e.g., promotion goals, relating to one's hopes, wishes, and aspirations, such as dreaming of a nice house, an exotic holiday), they consider affective information as more relevant than the substance of the message and, as a consequence,

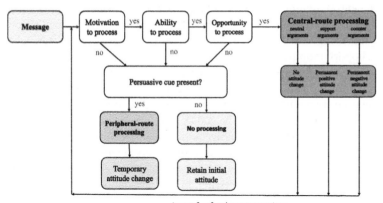

Input for further processing

Figure 3.2   Elaboration Likelihood Model

are more likely to base their evaluation on affect and follow the central route. On the other hand, when consumers' prevention goals, relating to one's duties, obligations, and responsibilities, such as providing for a child's education or looking professional at work, are their driving goal, the opposite result is found.

Any advertiser aims for reaching consumers in such a way that they process the advertising message centrally. Consequently, the advertiser has to see to it that the message reaches the target customers when and where they are motivated to process it, i.e., when and where they feel a need or a desire for a product, and approach them with messages that tap into the nature of this need (functional, hedonic, sensory...). Additionally, the advertiser should reach target groups such that they are able to process the message: use language they understand, and show contexts that are relevant to them and to which they can relate. Finally, advertisers should try to expose target customers to their messages in contexts where these customers can fully process the messages without distraction. However, often consumers do not process the message centrally, but rather periph-erally. In such cases, advertising will not work unless there is a peripheral cue that at least makes the consumers pay attention to the ad and may be partially persuaded by it. In other words, every advertisement should have "*stopping power*" by means of an element in the ad that attracts the attention: a beautiful model, a celebrity, a creatively made stimulus, an original approach, and so on.

There are several other dual-processing models that are more or less based on the same principle. According to Nobel Prize winner David Kahneman, people have a *fast thinking system* (System 1) and a *slow thinking system* (System 2), which roughly correspond to a subconscious and conscious system. System 1 helps us, for example, to quickly, automatically, and effortlessly recognize faces, speak our mother tongue with mindless fluency, and even drive a car on an empty road. System 1 is based on associative learning, gut feelings, habits, and heuristics, but it is not always appropriate or cannot handle all tasks. For example, to make a standardized computation in our head or to deliberate about advantages and disadvantages of an expensive purchase, System 2 will take over. So, the more rational System 2 checks on the intuitive System 1: but as this requires time and effort, System 2 oftentimes follows System 1. Also the *heuristic-systematic model* is conceptually based on the same principles.

Box 3.1   Research: driving brand engagement through sponsored posts on blogs and Facebook

A study investigated the impact of sponsored posts on consumer brand engagement (i.e., posting comments, liking a brand). The researchers wondered whether the effect of sponsored posts on brand engagement would differ depending on the social media platform on which the post appears (a blog versus Facebook) and on the objective of the campaign (raising awareness vs. enhancing product trial). Blogs are sought out for their content which usually implies that readers are motivated to thoroughly process the information. Using Facebook, on the other hand, is more driven by a motivation to connect with others and to maintain social relations, implying a lower motivation to carefully process information. In addition, distraction for a specific post is much higher on Facebook because it is embedded in a large amount of other posts and information resulting in not only low motivation, but also low opportunity to process messages. Second, raising awareness vs. enhancing product trial are two objectives that align with the first and last stage in the consumer's decision-making process, which typically involve increasing levels of motivation.

On the basis of 1,830 sponsored posts written by 595 bloggers, the researchers found results that are largely (but not completely) in line with the ELM. Sponsored posts with a low involvement goal (i.e., create awareness) were more effective when they appeared on Facebook, whereas campaigns with a high involvement goal (i.e., generate trial) were more effective on blogs. Blogger expertise – which is a peripheral cue – had a more positive effect on consumer brand engagement when the goal of the blog post was to raise awareness than when it aimed to increase trial. The peripheral cue, blogger expertise, thus appeared to drive engagement more for less important goals (awareness vs. trial). This is in line with the ELM and also with research that shows that early in the decision-making process source expertise is important, whereas in the later, more consequential stages, homophily (being able to associate with a source similar to oneself) becomes more important. This effect was found for blogs only though; source expertise failed to break through the low involvement barrier when the sponsored post was put on Facebook. To increase awareness on a blogging platform, managers should showcase the expertise and credibility of the blogger, whereas for creating trial both expert and novice sources can be featured.[1]

Based on the combination of how attitude formation is mainly built (cognition, affect, or behavior), on the one hand, and whether elaboration likelihood is low or high on the other, six types of advertising models can be distinguished (Table 3.1). Each of these types of model explains how advertising works, but under different conditions. In what follows, a number of often used advertising models of each type are discussed.

Multiple attribute compensatory models

The models that will be discussed here are relevant if the consumer's motivation, ability, and opportunity are high and especially when cognitive elements are important for attitude formation. Most of the time, when consumers take such a decision, they move through a "decision funnel," gradually narrowing down their choice options to finally arrive at a *choice set*, a limited number of options out of which they will actually choose. To make a choice, in this stage people will often resort to multiple attribute compensatory models. This means that they take multiple attributes (characteristics) of the product into account, and these characteristics can compensate for one another. For instance, a car may be somewhat expensive and not so beautiful (negatively valenced attributes), but they perceive it as very safe and eco-friendly (positively valenced attributes),

Table 3.1   Six types of attitude formation and change

		Elaboration likelihood based on motivation/ involvement, ability, and opportunity	
		High elaboration central-route processing	Low elaboration peripheral-route processing
Attitudes based on:	Cognitions	• Multi-attribute models	• Heuristic evaluation
	Affect	• Affect-as-Information model • Affect Infusion model	• Ad transfer • Feelings transfer • Classical conditioning • Mere exposure effect
	Behavior	• Post-experience model • Perception–Experience–Memory model	• Reinforcement model • Routinized response behavior

and the latter is more important to them than the former. The most famous and often-used multiple attribute models are the *Fishbein Models*. They serve as a framework for consumer research as well as a starting point for brand positioning and advertising strategy. The basic model is the Expectancy–Value Model that predicts attitude. The Theory of Reasoned Action builds upon that model to predict behavioral intention. Finally, the Theory of Planned Behavior adds a third component, and predicts actual behavior.

In the *Expectancy–Value Model*, brand attitudes are formed on the basis of three elements: relevant product attributes, the extent to which one believes the brand possesses these attributes, and the evaluation of these attributes or how good/bad one thinks it is for a brand to possess these attributes (also called "attribute importance"). More specifically, brand attitude is predicted by the weighted sum of brand beliefs and attribute evaluations:

$$A_o = \sum_{i=1}^{n} b_{oi} e_i$$

where

A_o = attitude towards object o

b_{oi} = belief of object o possessing attribute i

e_i = evaluation (importance) of attribute i

n = number of relevant attributes

In other words, since not all brand attributes are equally important for a consumer, brand beliefs are weighted by the importance that the consumer attaches to the different brand attributes. Table 3.2 shows an example of the formation of an attitude toward two car models A and B. To predict attitudes, a consumer study is set up (the results shown are for one person). Beliefs are measured by means of a seven-point Likert scale from −3 to +3. Attribute evaluations (importance) are by means of a seven-point Likert scale from 1 (not very important) to 7 (extremely important). This consumer appears to take seven attributes into account (first column in Table 3.2). Column 2 shows the relative importance this person attaches to each of the attributes. For instance, fuel efficiency is very important, while low price not so much. The third row indicates to what extent this person thinks car A possesses these characteristics. Apparently, this person thinks that car A is pretty cheap, prestigious, and eco-friendly, but rather small and not so safe. In the next row, importance and beliefs are multiplied and the results of this multiplication are added. This results in an "attitude number" for car A, in this case: 22. For car B, obviously the relative importance of attributes does not change, but beliefs do. This consumer thinks that car B is pretty safe, not overly expensive, and large enough, but not so fuel-efficient and rather mediocre on prestige and brand image. In the last column, beliefs and attribute importance are multiplied and then summed, leading to an attitude number of 10 for car B. Consequently, our consumer has a more positive overall attitude toward car A than toward car B. Since attitude is expected to at least partly predict buying behavior, on the basis of these results, there is a greater chance that the consumer will buy car A rather than car B.

How can advertisers use this information? First, they could try to add attributes that the consumer takes into account that are in its favor, for instance, the cool packs that come with the car (state-of-the-art navigation system, top-quality sound system …), all included. Second, brand and advertising managers could try to alter the relative importance of attributes in the mind of people. For instance, car A scores well on price

Table 3.2   An illustration of the Expectancy–Value Model

		Car A		Car B	
		Attitude toward cars A and B			
Attribute	e_i	b_i	$e_i \times b_i$	b_i	$e_i \times b_i$
Low price	2	+2	+4	+1	+2
Prestige	6	+2	+12	0	0
Famous brand	3	+1	+3	0	0
Fuel-efficient	7	+1	+7	-1	-7
Very safe	5	-1	-1	+2	+10
Eco-friendly	3	+2	+6	0	0
Large	5	-1	-5	+1	+5
Attitude			22		10

Notes: e_i is measured on a seven-point bipolar scale (1 = bad, 7 = good); b_i is measured on a seven-point unipolar scale (-3 = unlikely, +3 = likely).

and eco-friendliness, but these attributes do not seem to be overly important. Advertising campaigns can focus the attention on how important these attributes really are, and try to move them up in importance. Car B could try to increase the importance of price and car size. Third, campaigns could try to alter beliefs. Since fuel-efficiency and prestige seem to be very important for this consumer, both cars A and B could try to improve beliefs about these characteristics. Finally, both cars could position themselves by lowering beliefs about the competitor (for instance, by means of comparative advertising). For instance, car B could claim that it is a lot safer than car A (safety being a very important characteristic).

The *Theory of Reasoned Action* (TRA) is an extension of the Expectancy–Value Model. This model was developed to predict behavioral intention. The latter is determined not only by attitudes, but also by the subjective norm. A *subjective norm* is the beliefs one holds regarding what different reference groups (significant others) consider as socially desirable behavior, weighted by the consumer's need or willingness to behave according to the norms of the particular reference group. The latter is referred to as *social sensitivity*. An example of socially influenced behavior is that a teenager might not hold a favorable attitude toward smoking himself; nevertheless, he might do so because his or his friends regard it as "cool" to smoke. Reference groups act as a source of information, and as an inspiration for normative behavior and identification (imitation). People usually have several reference groups, such as parents, children, friends, celebrities, social media influencers, journalists, business people, or famous football players. Table 3.3 illustrates how a subjective norm can influence the choice between cars A and B. The reference group valued most highly is the friends at school, while the sensitivity or motivation to comply with the opinion of social media influencers is lowest. The consumer thinks that friends at school, parents, social media influencers, and journalists will think highly of car A, but friends in youth and sports clubs will not. The same person will think that journalists will like car B a lot, while most other reference groups not so much. Applying the same calculations as before, all this leads to a subjective norm of 35 for car A and 1 for car B. In view of these results (as well as the results in Table 3.2), the intention to buy car A will be much higher than the intention to buy car B.

The insights with respect to the subjective norms provide extra angles for advertising strategy. For instance, one of the car brands could try to add

Table 3.3   An illustration of subjective norm effects

		Subjective norm			
		Car A		Car B	
Reference group	ss_i	oo_i	$ss_i \times oo_i$	oo_i	$ss_i \times oo_i$
Friends at school	6	+2	+12	-1	-6
Friends in youth club	5	0	0	+1	+5
Friends in sports club	5	-1	-5	+1	+5
Parents	4	+2	+8	-2	-8
Family	4	+1	+4	0	0
Social media influencers	3	+2	+6	0	0
Journalists	5	+2	+10	+2	+5
Subjective norm			+35		+1

Notes: ss_i is measured on a seven-point bipolar scale (1 = low, 7 = high); oo_i is measured on a seven-point unipolar scale (-3 = negative, +3 = positive).

a reference group that would work in its favor, for instance, car dealers. Car A could try to increase the importance of influencers, since it scores well with this reference groups. Car A could try to improve the opinion of friends in sports clubs (or people who visit sports clubs) and the perception thereof with its target audience. Car B could try to do the same with friends in school.

The TRA has been further extended to the *Theory of Planned Behaviour* (TPB). This extension was necessary to be able to deal with behaviors over which people have incomplete volitional control. Indeed, behavioral intention can result in actual behavior only if the consumers themselves can decide to perform or not perform the behavior. Behavior also often depends on non-motivational factors, such as resources (e.g., time, money, skills, or infrastructure). For example, a consumer may be willing to go to work by means of public transport, but when he or she lives in a remote village in which hardly any public transport facilities are available, this may be difficult to do. Or, a consumer may hold very favorable attitudes toward buying a Lamborghini, but when she lacks the money, a cheaper car will be bought in the end. *Perceived Behavioral Control* (PBC) is the perceived ease or difficulty of performing the behaviour and it is assumed to reflect past experience as well as anticipated impediments and obstacles. Perceived behavioral control is computed by multiplying control beliefs (what could stop people from actually behaving in a way they intend to) by perceived power of the particular control belief (do I feel I have control in that I can overcome this barrier) to pose the behavior, and the resulting products are summed across the salient control beliefs. In the case of buying a car, this could mean: well, this car is so expensive that many people cannot afford it (control belief), but I think I can manage to find the money to overcome that (perceived power). PBC is about perceived barriers to purchase. The consequence for advertising strategy is that advertisers should not just send out messages that improve attitudes and subjective norms, but also identify barriers to purchase and remove them by reassuring people that they are not actually barriers or help them to overcome these barriers. For example, in the past, MasterCard used the slogan "North. South. East. West. No card is more accepted" to indicate you can pay everywhere with MasterCard. Nike stresses "Just do it," meaning that everyone can be an athlete.

The TPB has been applied to a variety of issues, from predicting fair trade product purchase to condom use, from intentions to promote women in a job context to car-pooling, from organ donation to suicide prevention, and of course also to buying products. In general, PBC and attitudes in particular seem to have predictive value, while the subjective norm accounts for only a small part of the variance in buying intention and behavior.

Heuristic evaluation

When one of the MAO factors is low, central-route information process-ing is unlikely to occur and consumers will probably process the com-munication peripherally, based on peripheral cues to form a cognitively based attitude. For example, when consumers do not have the time to compare all available brands on relevant attributes, they may infer from a high price that the brand is a high-quality brand and therefore form a positive attitude toward it. This process is called *heuristic evaluation*. They can also try to make inferences on the basis of ad characteristics. In other words, peripheral cues in the ad are used as a heuristic cue to evaluate the quality of the message and to form a general evaluation of the brand advertised. They seek for reassurance or credibility in heuristic cues such as brand name reputation, experts endorsing the brand, price level, or messages such as "already 10,000 happy customers." Another example is the use of celebrities. The heuristic in this case might be "if George Clooney loves Nespresso, it has to be good." Table 3.4 summarizes a number of ad characteristics that can be used as a heuristic cue.

Affect-as-Information and Affect Infusion Models

Affect has long been considered as a peripheral cue, having an impact only when people have low elaboration likelihood. However, it is increas-ingly recognized that affect may play a fundamental role in central-route decision-making. The *Affect-as-Information Model* posits that consumers may use feelings as a source of information to form an overall evalua-tion of a brand, not by means of a simple affective association, but in an informed, deliberate manner. According to this model, consumers evaluate brands by imagining the brand in their minds and asking them-selves "How do I feel about this brand?" Next, they infer like/dislike or

Table 3.4   Heuristic cues

Characteristics	Peripheral cue	Heuristic
Source	Attractiveness	The more attractive, the better
	Expertise	The more expertise, the better
	Status	The higher the status, the better
	Number of sources	The more, the better
Message	Number of arguments	The more, the better
	Repetition	The more, the better
	Layout	The more attractive, the better
Product	Price	The higher, the better
	Design	
	Brand	
	Country of origin	

satisfaction/dissatisfaction from the valence of their feelings. Consumers infer the strength of their preference from the strength of the real feelings that the brand evokes. A prerequisite of the Affect-as-Information Model is that when people inspect their feelings to judge a brand, they inspect their profound feelings in response to the brand. So, if consumers decide not to go to the movies, it is because the thought of going to the movies makes them feel unpleasant, not because they happen to be in a bad mood. As a consequence, for feelings to influence the advertisement or brand evaluation, they must be perceived as representative of the brand, i.e., consumers must be convinced that these feelings are genuine affective responses to the brand. Moreover, these feelings also have to be relevant for the evaluation at hand and match consumers' goals. When consumers' purchase motivations are hedonic rather than functional, the likelihood that they will perceive their feelings as relevant and follow the "how-do-I-feel-about-it" model is much more likely. Under high elaboration likelihood, people use their feelings because they believe they contain valuable information. When consumers closely scrutinize the arguments in an advertising message, ad-evoked emotions can be considered as an argument or a central cue. One way to elicit strong ad-evoked feelings is to make consumers think of pleasant things in the past, such as the birth of a baby, a wedding, a first romance, and so on. Another way is to use nostalgic ads. Nostalgic ads make use of music, movie stars, fashion products, symbols, or styles that were popular during a consumer's youth. Early experience performs a determining role in shaping subsequent preferences and actually can influence consumers' lifelong preferences.

Another – broader – model that tries to provide a framework for the role of affect is the *Affect Infusion Model*. It tries to explain how affect (mood and emotions) influences a person's ability to process information and how she responds to that information. The model distinguishes four situations on a continuum from routine to complex. In the case of a previously stored reaction to a familiar stimulus (e.g., a well-known brand or advertising campaign), people will automatically reproduce that action. In that case, affect will not influence processing and behavior. This mechanism can explain brand loyalty and routine buying behavior. To persuade people, it may be enough to just remind them of the brand they are loyal to or usually buy to trigger *direct action*. In *motivated processing*, an individual exerts a specific search strategy with a direct information-seeking goal in mind. Also in this case, affect will not have an impact on message processing and subsequent behavior. Think of a person looking for a specific car model and who is exposed to a car ad. In *heuristic processing*, affective processing occurs outside of one's consciousness. People make sense of their emotional reactions as they have them, including their implicit judgments. This is also known as the affect-as-information mechanism (see earlier in this chapter): the experienced emotion is used as information. In this case, mood and emotion will exert a substantial influence on message processing and behavior: think of nostalgic ads or ads focusing on emotionally involving situations. Finally, *substantive or systematic* processing, in other words, elaborate, complex, and/or novel processing, affect has the greatest impact on message processing and subsequent behavior, because mood can affect every stage of the cognitive process: attention, coding, recovery, and association. A consequence would, for instance, be that mood or emotions induced by a happy-ending movie would positively influence the response to a subsequent ad that requires elaborate processing. According to the model, anti-tobacco campaigns would be more effective if they emphasized the positive consequences of not smoking than warning about the negative ones. The basic consequence is that mood effects tend to be exacerbated in complex and novel situations, particularly in those that require substantial cognitive processing. In those situations, the affective context in which a message is received plays an important role: emotionally positive contexts would lead to more positive responses.

Attitude and feelings transfer, emotional conditioning, and mere exposure

The mechanisms in this section try to explain how consumers process ads based on affect in a low-elaboration context. Attitude transfer is the phenomenon that how one evaluates an ad may be transferred to how one evaluates the brand: "like the ad – like the brand and buy the product." When consumers feel indifferent toward the available brands as a consequence of low brand differentiation or insignificant consequences of a non-optimal choice, their choice goal is likely to be to buy a brand of which they like the advertisement. Peripheral cues such as humor, music, animals, and children may attract attention, induce curiosity which leads consumers to watch the ad, and induce a favorable attitude toward the ad that transfers to the brand. In line with the foregoing, the feelings an ad evokes may be transferred to the attitude toward the ad, the brand attitude and the purchase intention without much deliberation. People that experience positive ad-evoked feelings make decisions more quickly, use less information, avoid systematic processing, evaluate everything more positively, accept a persuasive message more easily and pay less attention to details. Since ad-evoked feelings and the brand are associated in a consumer's memory, thinking of the brand in another situation might activate the feelings associated with it. Emotional conditioning can be considered an extreme case of feelings transfer. Advertisers sometimes try to pair a brand with an emotional response. On the premise of a high exposure frequency and strong emotional content, attitudes toward the brands can be predominantly formed on the basis of emotional conditioning. Examples of brands that try to benefit from emotional conditioning are Martini and Häagen-Dazs (Box 3.2).

Box 3.2 Research: pleasant emotional ads make consumers like your brand more

In a Belgian study, the attitudinal responses of 1,576 Belgian consumers to 1,070 TV commercials shown on Dutch-language Belgian television over a three-year period were analyzed. This pool of commercials featured 318 national and international brands across 153 different product categories, including beer, credit cards, diapers, coffee, laundry detergents, cars, and computers. Groups of 20 to 30 respondents were shown sets of between 20 and 50 commercials and asked to rate them. After seeing each commercial, respondents rated their attitude toward the ad, how useful and informative the ad was, and their attitudes toward the advertised brand. Additionally, an independent group of judges rated the degree of emotionality of each ad and their degree of creativity. Another set of judges coded the 153 product categories represented in the ads in terms of their level of involvement and type of buying motivation (hedonic/experiential or utilitarian/instrumental) as well as whether the advertised product was a durable, a non-durable or a service, and whether the ad was for a search or an experience product.

The results show that ad-evoked feelings exerted a substantial influence on brand attitudes. Regardless of how creative or informative the respondents found the ads, their emotional content had a significant positive influence on their attitudes toward the advertised brands. Ads that evoke positive feelings are better liked, and better-liked ads lead to more positive brand attitudes. The effects of ad-evoked emotions on brand attitudes did not depend on the level of product category involvement. Products are usually bought either for fun (hedonic/experiential motives when buying products like ice cream or perfume) or to serve a rather functional purpose (utilitarian/instrumental motives when buying products like detergents or trash cans). The effects of ad-evoked feelings on brand attitudes were more pronounced for products typically associated with fun than with function. The effect of durables (e.g., cars and refrigerators), non-durables (e.g., food and toilet paper), and services (e.g., haircuts and phone subscriptions) was also investigated, as was the distinction between search goods and experience goods. Search goods can be easily evaluated by the consumer before a purchase (e.g., clothing and furniture), while experience goods can only be evaluated after the purchase, by consuming and experiencing the product (e.g., a diet program and movies). The results showed that product durability and the search vs. experience nature of the product did not influence the effects of ad-evoked feelings on brand evaluations.

Convincing a consumer to like a brand through advertising is mainly an emotional challenge. Advertisers should develop ads that elicit pleasant feelings because these ads are better liked and lead to more favorable brand attitudes, no matter which product categories are advertised. When advertising brands in product categories that are bought for fun, pleasure, sensory stimulation, and experience, evoking positive emotions is even more important for developing favorable brand attitudes.

Many studies have demonstrated that prior exposure to stimuli (nonsense syllables, words, slogans, pictures, faces, sounds, smells, etc.) increases positive affect toward these stimuli. In the same vein, frequent ad and brand exposures can increase liking of the ad and the brand. In other words, the mere exposure of consumers to a particular ad, without the consumer actively elaborating on the ad, can influence consumer preferences and behavior. Several studies indicate that the *mere exposure effect* on brand attitude is based on the fact that previous exposure to a stimulus can result in a more positive stimulus evaluation even if the respondent cannot remember having seen the stimulus before. Another explanation of the mere exposure effect is that prior exposure increases *processing fluency* at the time consumers have to make a judgment. The fact that consumers have been frequently exposed to a certain ad or brand results in a representation of this stimulus in consumers' memory. When consumers want to evaluate the stimulus later on (e.g., during a shopping trip), the representation of the stimulus in their memory will facilitate the encoding and processing of the stimulus. As a consequence, processing of the stimulus will be easier and more fluent. Frequent previous exposure to a brand or an ad leads to liking, believing or accepting the ad or brand, especially when consumers have been incidentally exposed to the ad or brand and are not aware of this exposure.

In today's cluttered advertising environment, consumers are frequently exposed to brand messages that only last a couple of seconds. This is especially true for online advertising. Internet users watch a couple of seconds of a removable pre-roll ad on YouTube, they are briefly exposed to retargeted ads, native ads in their Facebook feed, or banners on the side of the screen. These short ad exposures may well be effective because of the mere exposure effect: people are frequently exposed to a multitude of short exposure messages they do not remember afterwards. However, as a result of the omnipresence of the ads and the brand, this may result in increased fluency or increased perception of correctness, and ultimately, a positive brand attitude.

Perception–Experience–Memory Model

The models discussed above have often been tested for hypothetical or new brands. However, most advertising is for existing brands. The *Perception–Experience–Memory Model* tries to model what the role of advertising is for first buys and for other than first-time purchases. When consumers do not yet have brand experience, the main function of advertising consists of framing perception. Framing can affect consumers' expectation, anticipation, and interpretation. Expectation means notifying consumers that a particular brand in a certain product category is available and putting the brand in a frame of reference so that consumers expect to see it. Next, advertising should try to create anticipation. Besides expectation and anticipation, pre-experience advertising may offer an interpretation or a rationale for the anticipation the brand generates. For example, an unfamiliar computer brand could use the Intel Inside logo to assure consumers that it is a trustworthy and high-quality brand. A next critical function of both pre-experience and post-experience advertising is enhancing sensory and social experience. Products may taste better, function better, or look nicer, and the service may be perceived as friendlier or more knowledgeable just because consumers expect to experience this and anticipate the experience. A second role of post-experience advertising is to organize memory. It offers verbal and visual cues such as jingles, slogans, user imagery, and so on, enriching the brand schema and making it more likely that afterwards the brand will be recalled. Increasing brand recall and top-of-mind awareness can stimulate brand-switching. On the other hand, post-experience advertising may also prevent consumers switching to the competitor's brand. Finally, post-experience communications also help consumers to interpret their experiences: The advertisement not only influences the consumer to feel that the sensory or social experience was a good one, but it also provides reasons to believe that it was. In an era in which the majority of product category brands are converging instead of becoming more distinct, post-experience advertising may offer the extra element for a brand to be perceived as better, or more unique, than the rest.

Reinforcement and routinized response

In this case, at least one of the MAO factors is low, making well-thought-through processing less likely. Consumers will rather concentrate on elements of previous brand experience to form an attitude and purchase intention. According to the *Reinforcement Model*, awareness leads to trial and trial leads to reinforcement. Product experience is the dominant variable in the model, and advertising is supposed to reinforce habits, frame experience (see previous section), and defend consumers' attitudes. A similar model assumes that a large number of product experiences can lead to *routinised response behavior*, especially for low-involvement, frequently purchased products such as toilet paper, toothpaste, paper tissues, mineral water, or chewing gum. In this case, consumers do not spend much time on deciding which brand to buy, but buy a particular brand out of habit. In other words, previous behavior guides future behavior. Although the initial brand choice may have been thoroughly elaborated, routinized response behavior is characterized by very low cognitive effort in which very few possibilities are considered. Building and maintaining brand awareness and trying to become top of mind is very important here in order to be included in the limited set of brands that a consumer is willing to consider, to retain brand loyalty and to enhance brand-switching to the own brand.

The advertising theories discussed before all apply to a specific message processing context. Additionally, a number of frameworks have been proposed that provide a more comprehensive account of how advertising may influence behavior.

Cialdini's persuasion principles

One of the most famous frameworks of which basic mechanisms guide human behavior is Cialdini's six persuasion principles. The *Reciprocity* principle states that human beings are inclined to return favors and pay back debts, in other words to treat others as they expect to be treated themselves. For instance, if an online advertiser offers relevant content for free on a landing page (a webinar, an e-book), visitors will be inclined to leave their contact data (email address). The *commitment/consistency* principle means that people have a need to be seen as consistent. As such, once they commit to something or someone, they are likely to go through and deliver on that commitment, hence be consistent. For instance, by getting website visitors to commit to something relatively small and usually free of charge or at very low cost, like a guide or a whitepaper, the likelihood increases that those site visitors will eventually see themselves as customers. That change in self-perception makes them more susceptible to accept a paid product or service. This is the principle behind the use of a tripwire: first offering a simplified version of the product or service that is sold or "splinter" off part of a product or service as a separate low-threshold offer. The *social proof* principle holds that people are inclined to do what they observe other similar or influential people are doing. This factor is similar to the subjective norm effect in the theory of planned behavior, and explains the effectiveness of advertising techniques such as testimonials, celebrity endorsement, and influencer marketing. The *authority and obedience* principle states that people are inclined to obey authority figures. This explains the persuasive effects of expert endorsers and social media influencers, and why we see people looking like dentists in toothpaste ads and like plumbers in dishwasher descaler ads. *Liking* people increases the chance that you are influenced by them. Well-known and physically attractive or trustworthy endorsers make advertising more persuasive – ask Nespresso and George Clooney. Finally, *scarcity* is the perception that products are more attractive when their availability is limited. Think of "only two of these rooms left" in hotel ads or on travel booking sites, or "available at this price only this week."

The strong and weak theory of advertising effectiveness

The *strong theory of advertising* posits that advertising has the power to inform, persuade, and sell. It is the standard theory that has been adopted by academics and practitioners alike for many decades. Advertising is considered the driving force behind consumer behavior, and is assumed to be able to strongly steer this behavior. The HoE models are typically those that are embedded in this "strong theory" thinking. However, although these models may be handy frameworks to describe advertising goals in a campaign, there is little empirical evidence that customers actually go through each of a number of stages before buying a product.

Instead, advertising tends to work in the longer run, after an interaction between all these stages in the mind of the customer. For sure, advertising has been capable of building strong brands over time, but it is far less certain that this brand building has been accomplished as a result of short-term, step-by-step persuasion by advertising as suggested in the strong theory.

The *weak theory of advertising* posits that, instead of persuading people to consume products and brands and "guide" them through various consecutive stages of persuasion, advertising is only capable of gently nudging them toward a particular product or brand and afterwards remind them to become and stay loyal customers. It is highly unlikely that advertising alone is capable of successfully guiding customers through all stages of persuasion. The weak theory states that most buying behavior is rooted in past experience. Advertising can make people aware of a brand or a product. Advertising and the other tools of the marketing and communication mix (distribution, pricing, promotion …) can make people try a product and, later on, advertising acts to remind and reinforce a previous buying decision. This logic is called the *Awareness–Trial–Reinforcement* (ATR) *Model*. This model basically proposes that advertising reinforces positive associations with a brand that people have already adopted. Consequently, advertising reinforces the habit of existing customers and keeps them loyal. Big brands remain big because they have more loyal customers that buy more often, and this is reinforced by advertising; small brands remain small because they have less loyal customers that also buy less than those of bigger brands. This is also known as *"double jeopardy."* The weak theory thus states that advertising predominantly supports existing buyers, reinforces past sales and improves repeat buying.

How advertising works online

The purpose of advertising is always to carry over information about brands, instill brand value and positive brand perceptions in potential consumers, and activate consumers to react upon the brand, buy it, and become loyal to it. What is different in an online environment compared to traditional offline advertising are the tools used, and most of all, the fact that individuals interactively connect with one another and with brands on a much larger scale than would be possible in a traditional offline environment. Social media and social networks in particular facilitate this intense interaction. Consequently, online advertising works according to the *"pinball"* principle (see Chapter 2): throw in the ball (the ad and/or the brand) and try to keep it in the game as long as possible with the help of the pins (the customers) who engage with it and actively give it visibility and promote it.

A model as to how advertising works has been proposed to incorporate the impact of digital media and interactivity starts from the assumption that digital advertising works according to four different principles: Persuasion, Involvement, Salience, and Sales Promotion. The *Persuasion* framework is the classical one. Brands gradually move consumers through a sequence of stages to persuade them to buy a brand, based on rational benefits and a clear selling proposition. This is similar to what the traditional HoE models prescribe. In a digital context, the brand persuades consumers, not just by one-sided narration, but by "guided exploration." The brand encourages and helps consumers to explore and find out more about the brand. This can be done through brand pages on social media, electronic newsletters, online brand communities, and using content marketing to guide people to the digital sales funnel (ToFu (top-of-funnel), MoFu (middle-of-funnel), BoFu (bottom-of-funnel): see Chapter 4). The *Involvement* framework provides consumers with a brand-inclusive experience, sometimes rationally, but mostly emotionally. Advertising convinces the customer that the brand is valuable to them, because it holds shared or aspirational values. In the digital age, this involvement is deepened because consumers can be encouraged to "play." Consumers can create content about the brand, and partly take over control of brand building and brand communication. This user-generated content turns up in blogs and videos, on review sites, and social networks. The *Salience* framework assumes that advertising works when it is creative, original, and stands out. The brand is very salient in the minds of people when they pay attention to its exceptional and attention-grabbing advertising. In a digital context, this effect is amplified when people share these brand messages and discuss the brand online through social media. Finally, the *Sales Promotion* framework starts with the premise that advertising should be aimed at influencing buying behavior and driving sales. Messages are intended to drive participation in promotions, sales, price deals, and so on. The digital context has not fundamentally changed this framework. Digital advertising has always been aimed at provoking a behavioral response, including buying behavior. All in all, the digital context has provided new tools and new means to communicate with consumers and, most importantly, to activate them to communicate with the brand and with other consumers about the brand (Box 3.3).

Box 3.3   Research: how to advertise sales promotions on social networking sites

Sales promotions represent a category of brand activation initiatives aimed at increasing sales in the short run, both from existing and new customers, based on a temporary incentive and therefore used for a short period of time. Sales promotions can also drive brand-related engagement on social media. On these platforms, traditional promotional tools (e.g., coupons and contests) can get a new life, while emerging promotional strategies (e.g., branded virtual gifts) can arise. A Belgian study aimed to explore the determinants of the effectiveness of sales promotions posts with respect to what drives an increased customer engagement in terms of the number of likes and comments posts generate. Based on 156 promotional posts on Facebook and Instagram by Belgian fast-moving consumer goods brands, the study analyzed to what extent engagement with these posts are influenced by the type of promotion (i.e., monetary incentives, prize promotions, product promotions), the social media platform (Facebook and Instagram), and the types of textual appeals ("speech acts") in the posts. Speech acts represent words communicating the speaker's intent of evoking some behavior in the recipient. Firms posting sales promotions on social media commonly use two types of speech acts: they provide objective information to users, such as "Giveaway time!," "It is time for a contest" (declarative acts) and/or call consumers to action, such as "write a comment to enter the contest," "give us a 'like' to participate" (directive acts).

The study shows that, compared to monetary incentives or product promotions, the use of prize promotions leads to increased passive (e.g., likes) and active (e.g., comments) engagement with brand-related content. Instagram represents a context that fits better with the development of passive engagement levels (e.g., likes), but not with active engagement levels (comments).

Additionally, the results also show that posts on Instagram lead to better results in terms of comments than on Facebook. A positive effect from the number of declarative acts could have been expected based on the assumption that the higher their number, the higher the promoted deal's value perception. However, there was no effect from increased levels of declarative speech acts on liking and commenting behaviors. Also contrary to expectations, promotions using many directive acts reduce the likes and comments they receive.

Advertisers should thus keep the sales promotion proposition as simple as possible. Promotional offers should be highly directive, unambiguous, straightforward, without many mechanics or rules, and easy to opt-in, using only text that is necessary to explain the characteristics of the promotional offer in a non-ambiguous way. Second, promotions lead to more customer engagement on Instagram than on Facebook, making the former a better platform for sales promotion than the latter. Third, prize promotions in social media posts lead to significantly higher customer engagement than monetary incentives or product promotions. This effect is even stronger on Instagram than on Facebook. The general overall recommendation is thus to post simple, uncomplicated prize promotion posts on Instagram for the best engagement results.[2]

One of the fundamental differences between the offline and the online advertising environment is that the latter actively tries to engage (potential) customers to build brands (earned media) by capitalizing on the aspect of social interaction and identification. However, the reaction to brand messages in social networks will be influenced by the social context. Three aspects that determine responses to interpersonal communication have been identified: homophily, tie strength, and source credibility. *Homophily* is the extent to which individuals are alike and share, for example, the same age group, gender, education, lifestyle, social class, or interests. Perceived homophily increases the likelihood of perceiving the other as being more persuasive. Perceived homophily also stimulates a greater level of interpersonal attraction, trust, and understanding. It can serve as a cue to indicate that a product or service mentioned is suited, for example, to their age group or gender. As a result, information from a homophilous source (for instance, a post on Facebook) has more influence in the decision-making process compared to information from a heterophilous (dissimilar) source. *Tie strength* represents the strength of the interpersonal relationship in the context of social networks. Tie strength is characterized by the importance attached to the social relation, the frequency of social contact, the type of social relation, the intimacy between two parties, and so on. In an online social network, interpersonal tie strength could be reflected, for instance, by the number of common friends and shared activities, or the number of interactions between two people. Individuals in a strong tie relationship interact more frequently and exchange more information. As a result, strong ties are more influential than weak ties. Tie strength reduces potential risks, as stronger ties are perceived as more credible and trustworthy. Furthermore, perceived tie strength encourages users to interact and to spread information. In sum, tie strength between individuals should have a positive effect on consumers' responses to a message posted online. *Source credibility* is the degree to which a source is considered to be unbiased and/or an expert in its field. A person's knowledge on a certain topic, occupation, social training, or experience can contribute to whether or not they are perceived as credible. A message can be perceived as credible because the source has expertise and does not appear to have any self-interest to recommend the product. In this case, consumers will pay more attention to the message and it will be easier to persuade.

These three factors are thus important determinants of how people react to and interact with messages disseminated by others. Advertisers can take these factors into account to leverage the effect of their advertising campaign by means of viral marketing efforts that incentivize social media users to engage with brands and like, share, and comment upon branded content, and develop UGC themselves that reaches connections on social media that are similar to them, with which they have strong ties, and for which they are credible.

Notes

1. C. Hughes, V. Swaminathan, and G. Brooks (2019), "Driving brand engagement through online social influencers: an empirical investigation of sponsored blogging campaigns," *Journal of Marketing*, 83(5), 78–96.
2. C. Buzeta, N. Dens, and P. De Pelsmacker (2021), "Sales promotion posts across different social media platforms: a speech act analysis," University of Antwerp, working paper.

4 Advertising planning

This chapter discusses the advertising planning process and a schematic overview is presented in Figure 4.1.

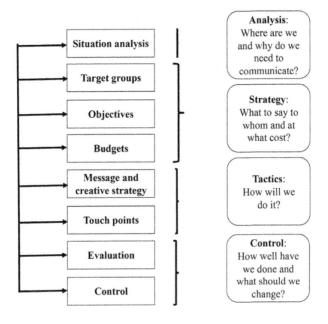

Figure 4.1   The advertising plan

Situation analysis

The first stage in the advertising planning process is a situation analysis of the current and future marketing context. Advertising has to be embedded in the overall marketing strategy of the company. The situation analysis is important because it enables the advertising manager to establish a solid base on which the advertising strategy can be built. The *situation analysis* provides the answer to the question: why do we have to communicate? The situation analysis needs to be a comprehensive assessment of the company, its products and brands, and its competitive and macro-environment. Elements that have to be investigated are:

- Markets: What are the market size evolution, market shares, market segments, consumer characteristics, and behavior; what is the basic consumer behavior insight on the basis of which we could build our message strategy?
- Products and brands to be communicated: What are their unique strengths and weaknesses, what is the unique selling proposition to be advanced, what could be the communication platform, i.e., the arguments with which to convince the target group, etc.?
- Competitors: Who are our competitors? What are their strengths and weaknesses, and their (advertising) strategies?
- Macro-environment: What are the political and legal restrictions or regulations, the economic situation, sociological concerns, and technological evolutions?

Specific analyses can be carried out to prepare the advertising strategy, such as the *advertising audit*, competitor advertising strategy research, advertising content research, and management judgment tests. In an advertising audit, all forms of advertising the brand currently uses (TV ads, online natives, outdoor, etc.) are screened to assess their consistency with overall strategy, as well as their internal consistency. The audit can be carried out on the basis of an internal analysis, but also target group members could be involved. On the basis of this advertising audit, the advertising strategy for a brand and/or instruments used can be adjusted. *Competitor advertising strategy research* screens competitive ads to judge competitive advertising strategies in order to define target groups and positioning strategies more clearly for the company's own products. In addition, competitive media strategies and media mixes can be studied to get an idea of the competitors' advertising budgets and shares of voice, target groups, positioning, and strategies. *Advertising content research* is used to help advertising creatives generate ideas about the content of new advertising stimuli. When a new campaign is to be launched, brainstorming sessions can be organized, involving creatives, advertisers, and consumers. *Thought-starter lists*, in which a multitude of potential benefits of the brand or product to be promoted are listed, may also be used to get the process underway.

Segmenting, targeting, and positioning

Consumers have different characteristics, different needs, and different ways in which they want to satisfy their needs. Therefore, companies have to find out in what way market segments are different with respect to their products and brands, which target markets to select, and how to approach them. Developing a strategy to sort this out is referred to as the *segmenting–targeting–positioning* (STP) *process*.

Segmentation

Market segmentation is the process of dividing consumers into homogeneous groups in that the members of one group should react in the same way to advertising stimuli and differ in their reactions to these stimuli from the members of other segments. In other words, it is not sufficient for men and women to be physiologically different. If no systematic difference between the two groups in the way they react to advertising stimuli can be expected, there is no sound reason to distinguish between them. Segmentation starts with a definition of potentially relevant factors on the basis of which a market can be segmented. Different variables or criteria can be used to segment a market.

Markets can be divided into different *geographic segments* such as countries, climate, nations, regions, or neighborhoods. Consumer behavior and buying patterns often denote cultural differences and therefore the place where consumers live may require other advertising approaches. *Demographic segmentation* divides the market on the basis of sex, age, family size, religion, birthplace, race, education, or income. These segmentation variables are frequently used, not only because they may correlate with other variables such as consumer needs, but also because they are less difficult to measure than others. Consumer markets can also be segmented on the basis of household life-cycle criteria. This concept is founded on the fact that family changes (e.g., marriage, birth of children and children leaving home, break-up of the marriage) affect both income and expenditure patterns of households. Consequently, each stage will have different needs. For instance, singles are an interesting market for entertainment and travel; newly married people need houses or apartments and furniture; families with young children spend a lot on baby care products and toys; and retired people have a lot of time to travel and for leisure activities.

Segmenting markets using lifestyle or personality criteria is called *psychographic segmentation*. *Lifestyle segmentation* describes how people stand in life, organize their lives, and spend their time and money. Lifestyle measurement is thus based on the *activities, interests, and opinions* (AIO) of consumers. Activities include how people spend their money and time, e.g., work, leisure, product use, or shopping behavior. Interests can be in fashion, housing, food, cars, culture, and so on. Opinions are attitudes, preferences, and ideas on general subjects such as politics or economics, on more specific subjects, or on oneself and one's family. These AIOs are also linked to a person's personality (e.g., a risk-averse person will not take up dangerous sports).

When a company divides its market into segments referring to product or brand preferences, involvement with categories, or buying behavior, it uses a *behavioral segmentation* approach. Consumers can be segmented on the basis of the occasion when they use a product or a brand. For instance, a brand of orange juice can be targeted at a segment of consumers drinking juice at breakfast, but there will also be a segment using orange juice in cocktails in the evening. Markets can also be divided into segments on the basis of customer loyalty. Customers can be loyal to one brand, loyal to a set of brands or brand-switchers. Brand-switchers are mainly influenced by material incentives such as sales promotions. Brand-loyals, on the other hand, do not have to be convinced. Advertising to keep the brand top of mind and offering loyalty promotions is called for to persuade these consumers. Consumers that are loyal to a set of brands will have to be approached with a combination of tools. Image advertising will keep the company's brand in their choice set, while advertising for sales promotions will make them choose the company's brand rather than competing brands.

Markets can also be segmented on the basis of the user status of customers. An individual can be a non-user, a potential user, a first-time user, a regular user, or an ex-user. Non-users are consumers who will never buy a product. Men, for example, will never use sanitary towels. An advertising plan should therefore avoid talking to them. Potential users need to be persuaded to try the product for the first time. Advertising, building awareness and attitude, offering trial promotions, and in-store advertising may convince them to have a go. First-time users should be converted into regular users. Advertising, building a favorable attitude and a preference for the brand, together with loyalty promotions, might do the job. Regular users should be confirmed in their favorable attitude and buying behavior. They may be approached by means of advertising and loyalty promotions. Markets can also be segmented on the basis of usage rate. Heavy users are of particular interest to a company because they make up the largest part of sales. Light users may be persuaded to buy and consume more of the product by means of special offers.

Segmenting on the basis of benefits looked for by consumers, e.g., a salty snack should be mainly crunchy for some, taste good for others, and not be expensive for a third group of consumers. A specific benefit for which a brand has a unique strength can be defined, and the advertising effort can be targeted at the customer group preferring that particular benefit. Finally, consumers can be divided into more homogeneous subgroups on the basis of their buyer readiness. When a potential customer is unaware of a brand, awareness-building advertising will have to be used. For a group of customers already aware of the product, attitude-building campaigns are called for. People who are interested in and like the product should be persuaded to try it by means of advertising promotions.

Next, segmentation variables can be combined to form segmentation profiles, for instance single women living in France who are interested in cycling and have never tried an electric bike before. Segment profiles have to meet a number of requirements to be meaningful. Segments have to be measurable. It should be possible to gather information about segmentation criteria and about the size, composition, and purchasing power of each segment. They have to be substantial enough to warrant separate and profitable advertising campaigns to be developed particularly for that segment. Segment profiles have to be attainable, i.e., accessible and actionable. The company must be able to identify the segment members and target the advertising campaign at them separately. Finally, market segmentation should be differentiated, and ideally lead to more homogeneous subgroups. These requirements are sometimes referred to by means of the acronym ADMARS (accessible, differentiated, measurable, actionable, relevant, and substantial).

Targeting

Once a company has identified and defined segment profiles, it has to decide which segments to focus upon. Therefore, segment attractiveness has to be assessed. On the basis of this analysis of attractiveness, the marketer will select a number of target groups to focus on. This is called *targeting*. Segment attractiveness has to be assessments based on consumer and competitor analyses and the company's relevant strengths. To evaluate segments, companies have to look at four elements: size and growth of segments, structural attractiveness of a segment, objectives and budgets, and stability of market segments. Target segments should be profitable, meaning that they should contain a sufficient amount of consumers that are able and willing to buy the company's product, and competition should not be too strong. Current turnover, potential growth, and profitability of segments are the first important conditions that should be evaluated for each segment. Structural attractiveness can be analyzed by using Porter's five-factor model: current competitors, potential entrants, substitution products, and the power of customers' and suppliers' influence. Some attractive segments may not fit with the strategic objectives or long-term goals of a company, or be inaccessible because of budgetary constraints. The choice of well-defined target groups should later on be reflected in the selection of advertising objectives, message strategies, advertising instruments, campaign execution, and touch point planning.

Targeting online

When they go online, people disclose a lot of personal information: the websites they visit, the things they like and share, the searches they conduct, the content they view, demographic and location information, and so on. Tracking consumers' online activities and using this information to deliver advertising targeted to the individual consumer's interest on certain platforms and websites is called *Online Behavioural Advertising* (OBA), or *Interest-Based Advertising* (IBA). Across all these online platforms, targeting is done via algorithms that make sense of the vast amount of personal data the platform collects based on the information users disclose online. This is called *programmatic advertising*: the use of software to buy digital ads. It uses real-time systems, algorithms, and rules to deliver the automated purchase of data-driven targeted ads. Ad allocation is based on a bidding process, the result of which is immediately applied in campaign roll-out: the algorithm assesses whether a person visiting a website meets the desired characteristics and displays the ad to that person within milliseconds (*real-time bidding* (RTB)). The disadvantage of RTB is that advertisers lose control over the presentation of their ads, including the websites and next to what content they appear, where on the screen they appear, how long the ad is presented, and who clicks on the ad (a real person, made-up identities, bots …).

The targeting options that search engines and social media platforms offer are largely based on the same principles and criteria, although their operationalization may differ per platform. In any advertising campaign, be it offline or online, advertisers start from the description of a target group and try to select media by means of which they can reach this audience effectively and efficiently. For instance, in traditional offline media, advertisers could define their target group as men between the ages of 20 and 30 who are interested in sports, and then select the appropriate advertising media (magazines, TV shows …) in which to place their ads. In fact, the same happens online: based on a target group description and an analysis of this target group's online behavior, online platforms expose target group members to the ads. The difference with traditional offline media is that, online, this process is faster, more flexible, more fine-grained, personalized and customized, and easily measurable.

An essential tool advertisers use for tracking and personalization purposes is cookies. A *cookie* is a small text file that is stored in a user's web browser. It includes a unique identifier which makes it possible to recognize the web browser on a later occasion. *First-party cookies* are cookies placed by the domain shown in the browser's address bar. Some cookies serve functional purposes; others can then be used to track visitors and use this information to develop personalized advertising. *Third-party cookies* are placed by a domain that is different to what is shown in the browser's address bar. Typically, search engines and social media place third-party cookies on a network of millions of other sites, called *publishers*. This enables them to track many other websites and their visitors and to collect more data than they already gather via the first-party cookies on their own platform. Search engines and social networking sites gather data about Internet users and provide advertisers with indirect access to these data by serving as intermediaries in the advertising personalization process. Websites agree to placing third-party cookies as part of their business model (earning money by placing ads).

In the current programmatic advertising context, search engines and social media know, amongst other things, which web shops a person has visited looking for, say, raincoats, and uses this information to enable advertisers to place ads about raincoats that "follow" this person around on the Internet (Box 4.1). These platforms realize that this may give consumers the awkward feeling that they are "watched" all the time. From 2022 onwards, Google plans to block third-party cookies on Google Chrome, following the lead of, for instance, Firefox and Safari. As a result, this type of behavior-steered advertising will no longer be possible. Instead, on the basis of other information it collects, Google is going to put consumers in groups called *flocs* (federated learning of cohorts), based on common characteristics and interests (for instance, young raincoat buyers in the Netherlands) without a direct link with individual online behavior. As a result, advertisers will then have to target a group, rather than individuals, just as they have done for decades with offline media. However, large platforms such as Google, several social media, and news sites still collect more than enough data through their first-party cookies to enable behavioral advertising solutions.[1]

In the following paragraphs, the targeting options of a number of social media are described.

Google's business model is largely based on *Google AdWords*. Companies and brands pay to have their website ranked at the top of the first search results page. Targeting is based on the relevance of keywords for a company's business: Google visitors get to see sponsored links (ads) on top of their search results list that ideally should match the information they were looking for on the search engine. For an advertiser, choosing the right keywords is thus vital. Keywords can be Broad (picks up any word related to the keyword an advertiser selects), Phrase (picks up the word when used as part of a phrase), or Exact (picks up only when that exact word is used). Broad match will expose the ad to more people, while the reach of Exact match will be smaller. A campaign typically needs a balance of all three in order to get the best results. An advertiser can also explicitly exclude certain keywords it does not want to be associated with. Google owns YouTube, and targeting on this medium works the same way as in Google AdWords. Similarly, an advertiser must think in terms of keywords that their target audience will likely use when they search for YouTube videos.

Advertising through social media can be very effective to better target both new and returning customers, use customer-generated content for ads, test ads in real time using platform analytics to determine best performing ads (see Chapter 5), and grow a company's fan base and sales. Basic targeting options are relatively similar across social media. For instance, on Facebook, customers can be targeted based on five criteria: location (to reach people in certain countries, communities, or places), demographic characteristics (age, gender, level of education, relational status, job, etc.), interests (hobbies, movie preferences, food interests, etc.), behavior (previous buying behavior, type of device used), and connections (with a person's Facebook page or an event). Another option on Facebook is *retargeting*. For example, let's say a person searches for a hotel in New York. She clicks on a hotel website, for instance the Hilton Hotel, and she leaves the website without making a reservation. Facebook places a pixel (an alternative for a third-party cookie) on that person's device when she visited the Hilton website, which enables them to send follow-up messages to get her to come back to their site, and/ or automatically send ads for something related to what she just looked at. From then onward, if Hilton has chosen this option for its campaign, on another website she visits, ads for the Hilton will follow her around. Those are retargeting ads. Facebook's *lookalike audiences* can be used to expand a person's reach from an existing audience. For example, one of a brand's audiences (out of three or four) is converting to hot leads or buys significantly higher than the others. A lookalike audience will let the brand "clone" that relevant audience so that Facebook will try to find more people with similar interests or characteristics and send them a brand's ads. Instagram is owned by Facebook, and basically offers the same targeting possibilities.[2]

Box 4.1   Practice: Deutsche Bahn encourages domestic travel using programmatic technology creatively

According to Deutsche Bahn, the German rail company, 72% of Germans travel abroad for their holidays, often in search for famous world landmarks. In 2019, Deutsche Bahn worked together with the advertising agency Ogilvy Germany and the image database Getty Images to encourage domestic travel. Starting from travel interests that people had listed on their Facebook profiles and looked for online when making travel plans, the campaign "No need to fly" used an algorithm that identified German locations that resembled the iconic international destinations that people were interested in. The algorithm then, using geo-targeting, calculated the flying cost from the user's nearby airport and compared that in real time with the €19 price of a train ticket to the lookalike location in Germany. This visual side-by-side comparison then popped up on the Instagram feed of travel enthusiasts and local influencers. More than 10,000 unique personalized images were compiled in that way. The ads led to a click-through-rate that was 850% higher than previous Deutsche Bahn summer campaigns, generated an impressive 6.61% conversion rate, resulted in selling two million rail tickets in two-thirds of the time it usually takes, and led to an increase of 24% in year-on-year revenue for Deutsche Bahn.[3]

On Twitter, target groups can be specified on the basis of location, demographics, language, the type of people they follow, interests, behaviors, and the events they are interested in. Audiences' interests can also be targeted by keyword. A company can also upload its own lists of people to target by their email address or Twitter ID or retarget people who visited its website. Pinterest also allows for different types of targeting. *Interest targeting* shows ads to people with specific interests as they browse their categories of interest; *keyword targeting* reaches people ready to act on what they find with Promoted Pins targeted to appear in search results and as related Pins. Keyword targeting helps increase in-store sales, boost traffic, and drive online actions by showing a brand's products to people ready to take the next step. *Audience targeting* shows ads to the people who are most likely to be receptive. Companies can target their website visitor list, customers in their CRM (Customer Relationship Management) system, or people who have already engaged with their brand on Pinterest. Much like on Facebook, a company can use "actalike" audiences to find other people with similar interests and behaviors. LinkedIn is a social networking site designed specifically for the business community. On LinkedIn, target group selection criteria include location, company name, industry and size, an individual's job title, function and seniority, their school, field of study, degrees, skills, gender, age, and groups they belong to. The *Audience Expansion* option automatically includes audiences like those a company have selected. Another option is to have the campaign delivered to the target audience *beyond the LinkedIn feed*, using LinkedIn's network of partner audiences.

On Snapchat, advertisers can use the *Predefined Audiences* option, where an advertiser can choose from over 300 pre-defined audiences based on what Snapchatters care about, what they buy, what they watch, and where they go. Advertisers can also select their preferred audience on the basis of demographics like age, location, device type, household income, and parental status. Snapchat also offers the *Audience Match* option, in which a company can combine its own data with Snapchat data to build custom audiences. As on other social media, the *Lookalike Expansions* facilitate building lookalike audiences similar to the company's best customers. TikTok offers targeting options based on gender, age, location (country, region, state, or province), app language, interests, and mobile device price (Box 4.2). TikTok can also create Lookalike audiences based on, amongst others, user engagement, app activity, and website traffic.

Contextual advertising or targeting is a type of targeted advertising that, instead of web visitor behavior, takes keywords and the topic and content of a web page into consideration to display ads. Contextual advertising is advocated as a tool which has the potential to solve the complex compliance issues now surrounding personal data (General Data Protection Regulation (GDPR) – see Chapter 6). For instance, on Google, the system analyzes the content of each web page to determine its central theme, which is then matched to an ad using the brand's keywords and topic selections, language and location targeting, and a visitor's recent browsing history. Contextual and behavioral targeting are not the same. Behavioral targeting is a targeting method that uses individual web user information and online behavior to place ad campaigns. In contextual targeting, automated systems display ads related to the content of a site based solely on keyword and the content of a site. For instance, if a visitor is reading an article about make up tips, there could be ads on the web page related to cosmetics and other fashion products. They are displayed on the basis of where the user currently is instead of focusing on where the user has been. Contextual advertising is based on the relevance of the environment rather than collecting user data to place targeted ads (i.e., behavioral targeting).

After segmenting the market and selecting target groups, a *positioning* strategy (a "place in the mind of target group customers") has to be defined. This will be discussed later on in this chapter.

Box 4.2 Practice: Nike uses TikTok to encourage young women to take part in sports

Because of negative attitudes, more than five in ten women in Milan don't engage in sports activities. To challenge these attitudes, Nike teamed up with TikTok to create dance challenge videos inspired by typically male-dominated sports like boxing, basketball, and football. The campaign, called "Nulla Può Fermarci" ("Stop at Nothing"), was developed with London agency AnalogFolk. It featured popular Italian female athletes and Milanese influencers who created dance routines that could be replicated by users. Each video included sponsored hashtags like #basketbeat or #theshadowboxer, and targeted young Italian women, encouraging them to express athletics through dance. More than 46,000 users responded to the dance challenge with their own dance videos, and over 300 media articles were written, including one that featured the athletes on the cover of Milan's newspaper, *Corriere Della Sera*.[4]

Objectives

Advertising objectives can be divided into three categories: *reach goals, process goals*, and *effectiveness goals*. The first goal of advertising is to reach the target groups in an effective and efficient way. For this purpose a good segmentation and audience definition are needed, as well as insights into the media behavior of the desired segments. For online advertising, this was discussed in the previous section. Considerations of offline media planning will be discussed later on in this chapter. Process goals are conditions which should be established before any advertising can be effective, such as capturing the attention of the target group, appeal to them or be appreciated, processed and remembered, and activate them. The third type of communications goals are the effectiveness goals. They pertain to the effect the campaign has on the brand: brand awareness, knowledge, attitudes toward the brand, sales, and profits. Basically, whether campaigns are online or offline, the same basic goals apply, although they may be termed differently for different media or platforms: draw attention, be seen, be remembered, activate, lead to positive brand effects, and ultimately commercial results. Advertising objectives can be further conceptualized on the basis of communications vs. behavioral objectives. This dimension refers to whether a campaign wants to change something in the mind of people or in customer behavior. Communication objectives aim at changes in knowledge or attitudes, while behavioral objectives want to change something in the way customers act. Based on these two dimensions, a taxonomy of advertising objectives can be drawn up (Table 4.1).

Besides a taxonomy for setting communications goals, this framework is at the same time a taxonomy of campaign effectiveness measurement. Indeed, campaign objectives and campaign effectiveness measures are two sides of the same coin. An effective campaign is a campaign that reaches its objectives. Setting objectives determines how effectiveness should be measured. Evidently, profitable long-term sales and market share growth are the ultimate objectives of most advertising campaigns. In many cases, commercial objectives will only be achieved after intermediary objectives such as reach, ad processing, and changing awareness and attitudes have been met. Reach goals should lead to sufficient exposure, process goals to enough processing and activation of the message, and communication effectiveness goals to the development of brand awareness and attitudes. It is generally assumed that campaigns first have to meet intermediary objectives before they can have a commercial effect. They are considered necessary conditions for longer-term commercial results. Consequently, besides commercial objectives, for most campaigns intermediary objectives are also set.

Advertising goals have to be SMART: Strategic, Measurable, Actionable, Realistic, and Timely. Advertising objectives are fundamental to campaign strategy: all phases of the advertising plan, such as creative, media, and budgeting decisions, should be built on the goals. As advertising objectives are also the criteria against which a campaign's success (or failure) is evaluated, it is important that they are well defined and quantified. Only when goals are measurable are they a management tool enabling returns to be gauged against investments.

One traditional model of effectiveness objectives and results measurement is the Defining Advertising Goals for Measured Advertising Results (DAGMAR) Model. The *DAGMAR Model* is a hierarchy-of-effects model that defines nine consecutive objectives: category wants, brand awareness, brand knowledge, brand attitude, intention to buy, purchase

Table 4.1   A taxonomy of advertising objectives

	Process objectives	Effectiveness objectives
Communication objectives	Brand recall and recognition Recall/recognition of message elements Attitude toward the ad	Brand awareness Brand knowledge: • Associations • Brand values • Positioning Brand attitude/image Brand preference Attitudinal brand loyalty Purchase intention
Behavioral objectives	Call freephone numbers Respond to mails Activation: • Store or website traffic • Likes, shares, and comments on social network sites • Talk or recommend to friends Capture leads: • Click-through on online ads to a landing page, a blog message, an app, a video • Collect information of target customers (email addresses, subscribe to newsletters, registration on website) Conversion: • Web shop visits	Conversion: • Trial purchase • Repeat purchase • Sales Market share Profit Return on advertising investment

facilitation, purchase, satisfaction, and brand loyalty. It is frequently used as a framework to select campaign effectiveness goals. In the following paragraphs, the nine goals are discussed. The first goal is developing *category wants*. In most cases, i.e., when advertising is targeted at category users, category wants can be considered as already present and thus can be ignored. However, in product categories that are infrequently purchased or infrequently used, such as painkillers, it may be useful to communicate category needs to remind buyers of their present but forgotten needs. Using category need as a primary advertising objective is, of course, a must for innovations in the form of new product category. Creating category awareness is also an appropriate goal when non-category users are addressed. The following advertising goals are not on a category level but focus on the brand.

Brand awareness is the association of some characteristics such as a brand name, logo, package, style, with a category need. There are three ways brand awareness can be defined. If people think of a soft drink, they may spontaneously think of Coca-Cola, Fanta, or Lipton Ice Tea. This is their top-of-mind brand awareness. People may also recall several brands spontaneously. This is brand recall or unaided spontaneous awareness. But it is also possible that people recognize a brand by its packaging, color, logo, and so on. This is brand recognition or aided awareness. If the purchase decision is made at another time and location than the point of sale (at the office, at home), or when a buyer has to ask explicitly for a certain product or service (e.g., at a drugstore or a pharmacist), brand name recall is needed. When the purchase decision is made in the store, and the buyer can use visual cues such as packages, displays, colors, and logos, brand recognition may be sufficient. To stimulate brand recognition, showing the product package or logo in advertising is crucial. To build brand recall, frequent repetition of the association between the category and the brand is necessary. *Brand knowledge* means that target consumers are aware of the most essential brand characteristics, features, and benefits compared with competitive brands.

Brand attitude is the perceived value of a brand to a consumer. Because a brand is stronger (and thus has more loyal customers) when the differentiation with another brand is bigger, brand attitude is an important advertising objective. When a certain brand attitude cannot be improved, it could be a strategic decision to develop a more positive attitude by repositioning the brand and perhaps find a better brand proposition for the targeted market (*rebranding*). Existing brand attitudes can also be adapted to appeal to other and new target groups or to improve attitudes with current customers. For instance, for a long time, the sandals brand Teva aimed at adventurous hikers who wanted "practical" shoes. In 2014, Teva embarked on a rebranding project with the motto "festivals are the new outdoor." The company asked several popular Instagrammers to wear Teva sandals at well-known festivals such as Coachella and Glastonbury. Several posts appeared on Instagram with the hashtag #TevaUpgrade, resulting in a more hip and trendy brand image.

The intention of the buyer to purchase the brand or the product or take other buying-related actions (going to the store, asking for more information, leaving contact details on a website, subscribing to an e-newsletter …) can also be enhanced. Especially in high-involvement situations, when perceived buying risks are high, the *intention to buy* is a necessary mediating step between a favorable attitude and the actual purchase. *Purchase facilitation* is about assuring buyers that there are no barriers hindering product or brand purchase. These barriers could be other elements of the marketing mix, such as price, product, and place (distribution). Sometimes availability or price is a problem, preventing consumers from buying a product. Advertising should minimize these perceived problems. For example, if a certain brand is not widely available in all stores, a list of approved dealers might help the consumers. Point-of-purchase communications may also help to facilitate purchases. The next goal is to stimulate *purchase*. In many circumstances it is difficult to use sales goals as a primary advertising objective, since advertising often works in the longer run. Nevertheless, there are situations in which stimulating sales could be a good objective, such as when a sales promotion is announced, in case of direct marketing campaigns, or in the last stages of an online campaign (see hereafter).

When the product or service lives up to the required and desired benefits or surpasses expectations, the consumer will be satisfied and thus inclined to buy the brand again. Satisfied customers are advocates of the brands they buy. Advertising should thus also be directed to developing *satisfaction* with new and existing customers. *Brand loyalty* is the mental commitment or relation between a consumer and a brand. Repeat purchase is not the same as brand loyalty. The former is often the result of habit or routine buying rather than of brand preference or brand loyalty. For instance, instead of evaluating alternatives and choosing a new brand for every new purchase, in low-involvement, fast-moving goods consumers tend to buy the same brands again without having a commitment to the brand. Next to focusing on higher market penetration rates, brands should also use advertising campaigns to retain their customers better, encourage their loyal consumers to use the brand more frequently, as well as suggesting new ways to use the brand or new situations in which it can be consumed.

Of course, not all advertising objectives should be present in a single campaign. Advertisers need a clear view based on situation analysis and prior research among the target audience to decide which goals a campaign should focus upon. The traditional DAGMAR model is a conversion model, i.e., turning non-users into users, whereas advertising is often directed at experienced consumers. Therefore, an alternative logic could apply: the *Awareness–Trial–Reinforcement* (ATR) *Model*. Advertising first arouses awareness, then induces consumers toward a first trial purchase, and then reassures and reinforces those users after their first purchase. Consequently, in this case, the goal of advertising is to create or recreate brand awareness and to nudge brand choice during purchases.

Online advertising objectives

Basically, the goals of an online advertiser, or the online component of an advertising campaign, are very similar to those of offline campaign components. After all, advertising is always about creating brand awareness, brand attitudes, generating leads, converting leads into buyers, and making buyers loyal. Those are also the main objectives of online campaigns. Often, three consecutive objectives are proposed:

> *Awareness*: reach enough relevant eyeballs (in online campaigns called "*impressions*") and get people's attention and interest, in order to generate traffic to the brand's website or landing page.
> *Consideration*: Capitalize on awareness by sending those people who landed on the brand's web page offers that will transform them from strangers into leads, for instance by retargeting them. The goal is often to get some basic information from them (for instance, their email addresses) by means of some kind of *lead magnet*, like giveaways, a checklist, an e-book or a webinar. For this reason, in this stage, ads should contain call to action (CTA) buttons, such as "sign up," "learn more," "download," "book now," and, of course, "shop/buy now."
> *Conversion*: Attractive offers are the next step to turn leads into customers. For instance, newspapers often invite readers to sign up to their online content for just 1 euro. This is called a *tripwire*, a simplified version of the big product or service that is sold. A company can also "splinter" off part of its product or service as a separate low-threshold offer.

When it comes to online marketing, this logic is often translated into the concepts *ToFu* (top-of-funnel), *MoFu* (middle-of-funnel), and *BoFu* (bottom-of-funnel) (Figure 4.2). They represent the different stages of the buyer journey, each of which requires the right content to be delivered at the right time to move the prospect through the funnel. At the top of the funnel, making the brand visible and developing awareness are the top objectives. The goal of ToFu content in advertising should be to educate a broad audience on a specific question or need that they're looking to address, but without an explicit sales goal. In the ToFu stage, typically *push advertising*, such as social media advertising, is called for. When a user sees a Facebook ad in their newsfeed, it's actually interrupting what they're doing. People do not like to be approached with a sales offer during their first interaction with a brand. They need to develop some form of relationship with the brand first. ToFu advertising should use meaningful content to develop a trust-based relationship with target consumers, such as a blog post, without attempting to specifically promote the company's brand or business. Once interested members of the audience reach out to the brand, they progress on to the MoFu stage. In this stage of the funnel, the advertising content should continue to educate but also begin to position the company as the solution to the needs and challenges of the prospective customers. The focus here is to convert potential customers to solid leads, by retargeting these potential customers by ads that aim at developing leads. At this stage, activating content is needed, usually an offer which trades premium content for an email address: introduce the company's brand, provide value for free, further build trust, and convert interested people to leads to email subscribers or activate them to go to the company's landing page or e-commerce site, again without sending a sales message to them. Finally, in the BoFu stage, leads should be converted into buyers by offering them activating content and compelling reasons to buy the company's product. This may also include sales or promotions of all kind (a free trial, or a discount). At this point, the leads pulled in through previous stages know the company and are comfortable engaging one-on-one. In this stage also *pull advertising* should be used, such as keywords buying on Google and YouTube. Since the user has already specifically established what they're looking for, the ad they receive is highly relevant. They "pulled" the ad their way.

Budgets

By means of *sales response models*, academics and practitioners have tried to depict the relationship between advertising budgets and sales. However, estimating the relationship between the two is not so simple and straight-

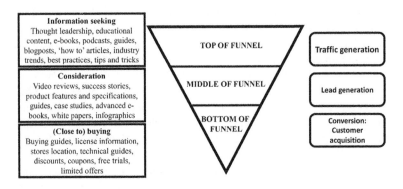

Figure 4.2   ToFu, MoFu, BoFu

forward. First of all, advertising is not the only marketing mix instrument influencing sales. Prices, product line decisions and changes in the distribution strategy will also influence them. Furthermore, an effective marketing mix implies that synergy and interaction exist between the various marketing tools. In a well-designed marketing plan each tool reinforces another. An advertising plan may lead to better results if the distribution strategy is optimized or the price is lowered. A rearrangement of the product line may result in more effective advertising and so on. As a result of this interaction, it is very difficult to isolate the effect of the advertising budget on commercial results. Furthermore, sales response models do not take the effect of competitive actions and environmental factors into account. Finally, advertising efforts may have both an immediate short-term and a long-term effect on sales and market share. That makes advertising budgeting based on "hard" calculations a tedious job. Consequently, management often employs relatively simple rules to set an annual advertising budget, or to decide upon a budget for a specific campaign. They are discussed in the following paragraphs.

The *inertia budgeting method* is to keep budgets constant year on year, while ignoring the market, competitive actions, or consumer opportunities. *Arbitrary allocation budgeting* means whatever general management decides to spend will be implemented. This technique is often used by small companies where the managing director's personal preferences (e.g., sponsoring a golf event) and contacts overrule more strategic processes that take the marketing and competitive environment and customer wants into account. In the *affordability method*, "leftover" resources after all input costs (i.e., human resources, operational, and financial costs) are invested in advertising. This method is often used in small and medium-size enterprises. In this philosophy, advertising budgets are considered to be a cost rather than an investment and are mostly not part of the strategic plan. In the *percentage of sales* technique, budgets are defined as a percentage of the projected sales of the next year. These budgeting methods are very popular in many companies due to their ease of use. They are mainly used to decide upon advertising budgets for a certain period (e.g., next year), and not for individual campaign budgets. Needless to say, all of them lack strategic focus. Inertia and affordability are very subjective ways of deciding how to spend advertising money and lack critical analysis and overall strategy. The affordability method ensures that advertising costs do not threaten profits, but suffers from the same flaws. The percentage of sales budgeting method could lead to overspending in markets in which these kinds of investments are not needed and at the same time advertising budgets might be too small where they might have had a major impact. Decreasing returns on sales will lead to smaller advertising budgets, which will certainly not help to change the negative sales evolution. Advertising budgets should not be the result of sales but rather should create demand and thus push up sales.

There are also advertising budgeting methods that have more strategic focus. One of them is *competitive parity budgeting*: companies look at the budgets competitors spend on advertising and base their budgeting decisions accordingly. First of all, they may simple copy the competitor's budget, based on the consideration that the collective behavior of a market will not skew much of the budget optimum. This method is often used in fast-moving consumer goods where sales are believed to be highly influenced by advertising spending. However, the underlying assumption is that the competitor's advertising budget was set in an effective and efficient way, and it implies that the resources, operational methods, opportunities, and objectives of competitors used as a benchmark are the same as those of the company itself. The method is also based on historical data and not on competitors' plans for the future. Companies can also base their budgeting decisions on competitive considerations without copying the competitors' budgets, when advertisers want to use their budgets to reach certain strategic goals. This implies decisions on *share of voice* (SOV) related to *share of market* (SOM). Share of voice is the ratio of own advertising investments divided by the advertising investments of all brands in the same product category or market. For instance, a company that wants to win SOM could decide to substantially increase its SOV for a certain period of time to overpower the competition. Finally, the *objective and task method* differs from the other methods in that they start from advertising objectives and the resources that are needed to reach these planned goals. All needed investments are then added and this will lead to the overall advertising budget. Budgets can be evaluated each year, and this feedback will lead to improved decision-making and more efficient budgeting in the future. The difficulty in this method lies in the estimation of profit impacts of different advertising tactics.

Besides these formal budgeting decision rules, a number of factors may influence the budgeting decision or may call for budget adjustments. For instance, sometimes it is necessary to make adjustments to the planned budgets during the year or during the campaign. If sales and profits lag behind projected and budgeted figures (planning gap), higher advertising efforts may be necessary. Crisis situations such as troubles with production or distribution might need exceptional investments in crisis communications. Unexpected opportunities or threats in the market might change strategic plans and advertising budgets, as well as unexpected moves by competitors (e.g., new product launches or aggressive promotional actions), new legislation, new media, and changes in media costs.

Budgeting online

Offline and online campaigns are similar in that in both cases companies have to decide upon a budget they want to spend, and allocate that budget as efficiently as possible across media, keeping their advertising targeting and objectives in mind. However, in most traditional advertising media, this means optimizing the number of "eyeballs" reached. Further, prospective customers should be activated and converted to actual customers. In traditional offline campaigns, reaching these goals often requires different types of campaigns with different communication instruments, for instance direct marketing for generating and activating leads, and sales promotions to generate trial and repeat purchases. Online advertising enables companies to reach all these goals by building campaigns that guide prospective customers through the entire sales funnel, from reaching them, creating awareness and interest, to activating them and turning them into leads, to converting them and closing the sale. Online advertising is much more flexible than offline campaigns. Companies can set a total budget, but also a daily budget over a given period. Different ads for different target groups and different objectives that are different over time are relatively easy and cheap to produce. Since online advertisers can keep track of campaign effectiveness in real time, they can easily and quickly remove the ads that do not work and replace them with new ones.

The way the online advertising budgeting is done is different from offline advertising, and sometimes also varies between online platforms. Given the advertiser's objectives and target groups, each platform's algorithm uses all the information it has from the platform's users to optimize campaign effectiveness, i.e., reach the advertiser's goals as well as possible, with the chosen target groups. All platforms have extensive management modules, dashboards by means of which a campaign can be organized: target groups, objectives, budgets, ads, and measurement of results.

The pricing model of Google AdWords and YouTube is based on a bidding procedure. Advertisers bid money for clicks. The bid sets how much an advertiser is willing to pay for each click. If the advertiser's maximum bid is, say, \$2, Google will only show her ad to people if other brands or companies are not bidding more. All this happens within split seconds. Google counts the clicks on an advertiser's ads and charges the company for each click. This is called *pay per click* (PPC). They also count impressions, which is the number of times an ad has been shown to users searching for the keywords an advertiser has selected. Clicks divided by impressions is the *click-through-rate* (CTR). This is the percentage of users who land on the page advertised because they clicked on an ad. However, the highest bid does not always win. Google combines the money factor with a quality factor in order to create the best experience for the user, since Google prefers to show its users relevant and better ads by someone who pays less, because that keeps users coming back to Google. To decide if and when to show an ad, Google combines the bid with a *quality score* – this metric combines several factors in order to determine how "good" an advertiser's offer is for someone's search. To obtain this quality score, several factors are taken into account, such as the *relevance* of the keywords for the ad and historical and expected CTRs. Next, *account history* is considered. Google determines if an advertiser represents a legitimate, credible brand with good products and services. Another important factor is the *landing page*, the place people will go once they click on an ad, which needs to be user friendly, attractive, and easy to navigate. Quality score and bid are then combined into *Ad Rank*. Ads with the highest Ad Rank appear higher in the list of its keywords. The pricing mechanism is the same for YouTube ads.

Pricing on social media platforms can be based on *cost per impression*, usually expressed as CPM (the cost per 1,000 exposures), *cost per click* (CPC), or *cost per action* (CPA), i.e., leads and acquisitions (acquire a customer), whichever objective the advertiser considers relevant for a specific campaign. On the platform's ad manager module, an advertiser can select an objective so that the platform based on the data it can use will automatically optimize exposure schedules. For example, if the advertiser selects "clicks," the platform will monitor and adjust in order to get the most clicks. If she chooses conversions, the platform will watch patterns for what's working (like what types of people, what times of day, etc.) and help self-correct the campaign as it runs. Within this logic, for instance, Facebook offers two bidding options, either "automatic," which means that Facebook determines the bid to reach the desired clicks at the best price, or "manual," in which case the advertiser enters a bid (for instance $1 per click) herself based on how much clicks are worth to her. Most platforms also allow determination of how much an advertiser want to spend per day or per week, and even the time of day. Finally, the advertiser can also determine how frequently she wants ads shown, for instance as quickly as possible during the day, or spread out evenly throughout the day. Budgeting on Twitter is roughly similar. An advertiser can try to increase the number of followers, traffic to his website, and/or leads. This means that, just like on Facebook, the advertiser has to decide the value of a new follower, lead, or click-through to his website and place a bid. The total and daily budgets can be adjusted based on advertising performance metrics and objectives.

Advertising on LinkedIn is also based on a bidding procedure. There are three options: CPC, CPM, or cost per send (CPS). *Cost per send* (CPS) is used when a brand runs sponsored mail campaigns, and pays for each mail that is successfully delivered. The CPM model is typically used when brand awareness is the goal. CPC is often used for action-oriented campaigns like lead generation or event registration. Companies have to select CPS, CPC, and/or CPM, and their suggested bid, daily budget, start date, end date, and total budget. They can cancel their campaign at any time. LinkedIn suggests a bid range to reach the company's objective, and gives a range of the current bids of other advertisers. The suggested bid range will be higher for target groups that are in demand and that many companies are bidding on. For all LinkedIn advertising products, bidding works as a second-price auction. That means if a company wins the bid, it will only pay the minimum needed to beat the second-highest bidder. LinkedIn determines who wins the auction based on the highest bid combined with past ad performance. Ads receive relevance scores based on factors like CTR, comments, likes, and shares. Campaigns with higher relevance get a boost in the auction process. The more relevant the ad, the lower the price a company has to pay.

Message and creative strategy

Message strategy

Once the communication context is analyzed, target groups and objectives have been established, and the advertising budget has been decided upon, a communication strategy has to be developed. This strategy should answer the question: what is to be communicated, and how? In other words, a message and a creative strategy should be developed.

What are we going to say to the consumers? The *message strategy* or *advertising platform* has to convince consumers. They have to know why they should buy the product, to learn in what way it is special, how it is beneficial or advantageous for them, how it can help them, and what characteristics it has or what benefits and value it offers. In order to answer the question "what is to be communicated?" a thorough understanding of the target group (*"customer insight"*) is crucial: what can the product do for the target group, what can the product mean to them and how can the product help the consumers reach their goals? Some customers see a car just as a functional vehicle, a means of getting them from A to B. This target group can perhaps be convinced by communicating the brand's attributes (airbag, engine, etc.) or benefits (reliability, safety, etc.). Other customers do not want to buy a car; they want to buy an image, a status. Obviously, the advertising messages to the latter group should be different from those to the former group.

Positioning

Preferably, the brand has to define a unique and relevant position for its products in the mind of the target group. *Positioning* is determining the way a brand is perceived by the target group on an important attribute, benefit, or value, the "place in the mind" a brand occupies relative to its competitors. Positioning attempts to claim exclusive "ownership" of an attribute, benefit, or value in the mind of the customer which differentiates it from the competition. Mercedes stands for luxury, Volvo for safety, Miele (dishwashers, washing machines, etc.) for quality, Levi's for the original American jeans, and Duracell batteries for power. The unique characteristic of a brand can be functional or symbolic. A functional benefit, also called a *unique selling proposition* (USP), refers to functional superiority in the sense that the brand offers the best quality, the best service, the lowest price, the most advanced technology. For example, Gillette is "the best a man can get"; there is "no better washing machine" than Miele; Durex "gives the most natural feeling"; "no card is more accepted than MasterCard", etc. A symbolic benefit usually reflects a unique psychological association to consumers and is referred to as an *emotional selling proposition* (ESP). You buy L'Oréal because "you are worth it" and you buy Nike because you "just do it." Other examples of brands that are promoted on the basis of symbolic benefits include Porsche and Louis Vuitton. A brand's advertising message platform should thus reflect the core positioning a brand wants to establish in the mind of its target customers.

There are a number of positioning strategies that a company can use, for instance a unique attribute (e.g., low-fat, the cheapest) or a unique benefit (e.g., the safest, the healthiest). A price/quality positioning means offering the same or better quality at a lower price than competitors. Positioning by use or application implies emphasizing a specific use or application of the product. For instance, Kellogg's introduced cereals as a snack at hours other than breakfast by offering little variety packets that kids can take to school. Comparative positioning is comparing a brand's added value against another brand in the same product category. For instance, Eurostar offers a fast train connection to London from France, Belgium or the Netherlands as an alternative to airline connections. Positioning by product user is associating a product with a specific group of users, e.g., Aquarius, a thirst-quenching isotonic drink for sporting men and women. Cultural symbols refer to brand personalities or branding devices such as Tony the Tiger (Kellogg's Frosties), Mr. Clean, and Captain Iglo. Not all differences with competitors are meaningful for an effective differentiation. The chosen USP(s) should be important to the target group, clearly different from what a competitor is offering, superior, easy to communicate, difficult to imitate or copy, affordable for the target group of consumers, and profitable for the company. Sometimes, a company can use more than one USP and/or ESP. Volvo, for example, claims to be both safe and durable. However, the more claims a company makes about its brands, the greater the risk of disbelief. Moreover, the different product benefits should be compatible in a consumer's mind: a super-strong detergent that also claims to be mild for the hands will not have any credibility.

Creative strategy

After the campaign message strategy has been established, a *creative strategy* has to be developed. The core message has to be translated into a creative idea and concrete advertising formats. Developing a creative idea and creative formats is the core task of an advertising agency. Before the agency can start thinking of a creative strategy, the advertiser must give the agency a creative brief. The *creative brief* should contain information on the target group, advertising objectives, and message strategy, but also sufficient information concerning the background of the company, the product, the market, and the competitors. Some examples of necessary elements are the long-term company and brand strategy, past, current and desired positioning, former advertising campaigns, message strategies and execution styles, desired media, available budget, and timing of the different steps (creative idea, execution strategies, campaign running, etc.).

The first step of the creative strategy is to develop a creative idea. A *creative idea* is an original and imaginative thought designed to produce goal-directed and problem-solving advertisements and commercials. A creative advertising idea has to be attention-grabbing and should lead to immediately understanding of the brand's position. In essence, a creative idea boils down to a proposition which makes it possible to communicate a brand's position in an original, attention-getting, but easy-to-catch way. Based on the core creative idea, creative formats have to be developed that "translate" this idea into concrete ads (TV ads, native ads, etc. – see Chapter 2).

Once a message and creative strategy has been established, campaign developers have to decide on how to get in touch with the target groups and which media to use to create touchpoints with them in a consistent and synergetic way. These media will have to be combined in an integrated advertising campaign. Finally, after the campaign is over, its effectiveness needs to be assessed and the results of this evaluation are going to be used to develop further campaigns and/or adapt current campaigns. Media planning is discussed in the next section. Campaign evaluation and results measurement are discussed in Chapter 5.

Media planning and selection

The cost of buying advertising time and space makes up a large part of the advertising budget. A *media plan* is a plan specifying which media and vehicles will be purchased when, at what price, and with what expected results. Media planning means selecting the appropriate media, given the target group of the advertising campaign and the characteristics of the different advertising media. Both qualitative criteria and quantitative media objectives for selecting the media mix are important. Media planning encompasses both offline and online media. The specific issues in online media planning have been discussed before in this chapter. The following sections mainly focus on offline media planning.

Qualitative media selection criteria

Qualitative criteria to evaluate different media are the extent to which the medium is capable of building a brand image and a brand personality, generate leads, convert members of the target group into customers, how involved the audience are with the medium, and, as a consequence, whether the audience are active or passive and whether or not the audience pays a lot of attention to the messages conveyed by the medium. Qualitative criteria are also about whether or not the vehicle can add value to the brand or product due to the context in which the brand or product is shown, how much and what type of information can be conveyed to the consumer (e.g., can the use and customer friendliness of the product be demonstrated?), whether or not the medium is characterized by a lot of advertising clutter resulting in a need for more exposures in order to become reasonably effective, whether the advertising message can be adapted for different target groups, whether the medium is more effective during certain periods of the year than during others (seasonal effects), and how expensive the production of advertising stimuli for a medium is. Additionally, the different media and vehicles must be considered in conjunction with each other. Is it wise, for instance, to plan the TV campaign after the radio campaign, or vice versa? Is it better first to explain the message in more detail in magazines before the out-of-home campaign starts? How important is it to have several TV commercials during prime time in the first week of the launch of a new product? Which radio channel does a target consumer listen to in the morning? Which billboards does he or she come across on the way to work? Which magazines or newspapers are read in the evening? Which TV programs are watched in the evening? Which online platforms create the best CTR and conversions? Often these qualitative criteria are first used to select media types (TV, print, online, but not radio, for instance), after which quantitative criteria are used to develop the actual media plan. Table 4.2 provides an overview of the characteristics, strengths, and weaknesses of a number of advertising media types.

Quantitative media planning objectives

After media types are determined, specific advertising media vehicles have to be selected. This selection is based on the media usage behavior of the target audience. Which TV or radio programs do they listen to or watch, at what time and on which days? Which newspapers and magazines do the target consumers read? Do they go the cinema? Media planning is based on databases in which the media usage of different types of target groups is documented. On the basis of this information, advertising budgets are allocated to ensure a maximum reach and frequency of exposure to ads for the budget. Considerations that play a crucial role in this planning process are frequency of exposure (repetition), reach, weight, cost, and scheduling. It is important to understand that, in media planning, reach and frequency is estimated on the basis of whether or not, and the number of times, one could be exposed to the media vehicle (a newspaper, a radio station), and not to the message itself. For example, if a consumer has a newspaper subscription and a certain campaign has one ad per week for six weeks in that newspaper, we know that the particular consumer will be exposed to the content of the newspaper six times during the six-week period. However, if the consumer does not always read the full newspaper and occasionally omits the pages in which the ad appears, the actual number of times he or she will be exposed to the message will be lower than six.

Table 4.2   Advertising media and media planning criteria

Media type	Strengths	Weaknesses
Outdoor	Wide reach High frequency Long message lifetime Immediate reach Geographically flexible	Low involvement Low attention potential Limited amount of information No context
Magazines	Selective on specific target groups High-quality context High involvement Quality of reproduction Lot of information Long message life	Long lead time Geographically inflexible Sometimes high clutter
Newspapers	Wide reach Short lead time Flexibility High involvement Strong context Lot of information Geographical flexibility	Limited selectivity Lower quality of reproduction Short message life
Door-to-door	Geographically flexible High reach Lot of information Promotion-orientated	Limited selectivity Low involvement Lower quality of reproduction High clutter
Television	Flexible Strong (emotional) impact Ideal for transferring image Supportive context High reach Selective	High production costs Very short message life High clutter Strong seasonal variation
Cinema	Very strong emotional impact Attention-grabbing Positive context Selective to young and upmarket target groups	Limited reach Slow reach Very short message life High production costs

Media type	Strengths	Weaknesses
Radio	High reach High frequency Low production cost Flexibility Very selective	Very short lifetime Low involvement Low attention Activating Brand building
Digital	Cost-efficient Flexible Brand building Activating/interactive High reach High frequency Potentially strong context Selective Measurable	Potentially intrusive Low involvement Low attention Clutter

Frequency

Frequency indicates how many times a consumer of the target group, on average, should be exposed to the advertiser's message within a specified time period for it to be effective. According to the *two-factor model*, an inverted-U relationship exists between the level of exposure, on the one hand, and advertising effectiveness (memory, attitudes, purchase), on the other. Wear-in and wear-out effects explain the nature of this relationship. At low levels of exposure, consumers develop rather negative responses (e.g., counter-arguments) due to the novelty of the stimulus. After a few exposures, the reaction becomes more positive. This is referred to as *wear-in*. More frequent exposures again lead to more negative responses, a phenomenon called *wear-out*. Negative responses, such as irritation, can be expected to be the highest both at low and high exposure levels, while positive responses are optimal at intermediate exposure levels. One way to counter or delay the wear-out effect is to make minor changes to the ad so that the consumer is not exposed to the same ad over and over again, or to use executional cues that evoke positive emotional responses.

The difficulty is to determine the optimal frequency level. This is linked to the advertising objective, the type of message used, media clutter, the product category, the competition level, the target group, and the media used. For instance, more complicated ads may show a longer wear-in and a postponed wear-out; humorous ads may have a short wear-in and a quick wear-out. An important question is which is the *effective frequency*, the minimum number of exposures, within a purchase cycle, considered necessary to motivate the average prospect in the target audience to accomplish an advertising objective. A common assumption is that a member of the target group is reached "effectively" only after three contacts. However, one exposure may be sufficient if the consumer is reached at the right moment, with the right message. For example, a consumer is driving home from work and a stone shatters the car window. One ad for Carglass mentioning that it repairs car windows 24 hours a day may be very effective at that moment. On the other hand, a consumer may need to see a yoghurt ad 15 times before it becomes effective. Moreover, two exposures may be sufficient for market leaders or an established brand image, while more might be necessary for new campaigns targeted at infrequent users, if the objective is to increase the usage of a product or when medium clutter is high. In other words, situational variables play an important role. In terms of media types, on average, cinema needs fewer exposures than television, followed by printed media (newspapers and magazines). Radio and outdoor advertising need the highest level of repetition. This difference is due to the nature of the medium type (audio-visual vs. only audio or only visual, for instance), and the way in which people are using or exposed to the medium. For instance, people do not always listen to the radio; often the radio is just "on." People pass by an outdoor billboard, but often do not pay close attention to it.

Reach and weight

To understand the relationship between frequency, reach, and weight of a campaign, a number of key concepts need to be explained first.

Total reach of a medium vehicle is the number of people who are exposed to the medium vehicle during a specified period, for instance how many people read *The Guardian*. Total reach determines the cost of advertising in that particular medium vehicle. *Useful reach of a medium vehicle* is how many consumers from the target group are exposed to the medium vehicle. Again, only exposure to the medium vehicle can be measured, not exposure to the message itself. Even within the same medium type, total and useful reach can differ substantially for different media vehicles. The greater the overlap between total and useful reach of a medium, the more selective the medium is and the lower the cost per useful contact will be.

Total and useful reach are medium-specific. Net and gross reach indicators are characteristics of a campaign (multiple media). *Net reach*, often referred to as just "reach," is the total number of target group members

Table 4.3   Reach and frequency distribution

Exposures	Reach as percentage of target group
1	20.0%
2	16.0%
3	11.5%
4	6.0%
5	3.5%
6	1.8%
7	1.2%

that are reached by all media used in a campaign. Some of these target group members will be reached several times, because they have been reached several times by means of the same or different media vehicles. For instance, a person can be reached three times because the ad was placed three times in a newspaper she reads, or she can be reached three times through one newspaper and two different magazines. *Gross reach* is the total number of contacts a campaign has made, duplications included. This represents the *weight* of a campaign. It is often expressed as *Gross Rating Points* (GRP): gross reach as a percentage of the target group. GRP can exceed 100%. Often, "%" is not added. These GRP can be realized by means of the same or different media vehicles. Another measure often used by media planners is *Opportunity to See* (OTS). OTS is defined as the average frequency (number) of exposure that an average reached target consumer has. It is calculated by dividing gross reach by net reach. Finally, *effective reach* is the number of target consumers who were potentially exposed to the advertiser's message at least three times. Suppose an advertising campaign reached 60% of its target consumers with the frequencies reported in Table 4.3. In this example, percentage net reach is 60% (20% + 16.0% + 11.5% + 6.0% + 3.5% + 1.8% + 1.2%). GRP is 147.2. Consequently, OTS is 2.45 (147.2/60). If the consumer needs to be exposed at least three times to be effective, then the effective reach is 24.0% (11.5% + 6.0% + 3.5% + 1.8% + 1.2%).

Cost

The *cost* of a medium is usually expressed as the *cost per thousand people reached* (CPM). CPM is calculated by dividing the cost of the medium (the air cost of a 15- or 30-second commercial, the cost of a one-page magazine ad, the cost of reaching 1,000 people seeing an online ad, etc.) by the medium's audience. More relevant is the *cost per thousand in the target market*, represented by CPM-TM. In this case, the cost of the medium has to be divided by the useful reach. The cost per useful contact is strongly related to *medium selectivity*, the extent to which a medium proportionally reaches a certain target group better. An example is given in Box 4.3.

Box 4.3   Practice: calculating cost per thousand useful contacts

Suppose a fashion chain wants to reach young females (between 16 and 30 years of age). An ad is inserted in three women's magazines, in a TV guide, and in a special interest magazine. The following CPMs can be calculated. Although the CPM for the TV guide is the lowest, calculation of the CPM-TM shows that, for reaching the young female audience, *Woman I* may be more cost efficient.

Table 4.4   Calculating cost per thousand useful contacts

Type of magazine	Magazine	Cost (€)	Total reach (000s)	CPM	(Useful) reach	CPM-TM
Women's magazines	Woman I	3,250	230	14.13	115	28.26
	Woman II	1,995	116	17.19	58	34.39
	Woman III	1,800	106	16.98	53	33.96
TV guide	TV One	3,900	585	6.67	117	33.33
Special interest	Modern Lifestyle	2,260	44	51.36	7	322.8

Media planning aims at maximizing (effective) reach, frequency, and weight of a campaign for the budget. However, given a certain advertising budget, reach and frequency cannot be increased at the same time. Both reach and frequency can only be increased by increasing the campaign budget. Media planning is a matter of finding the right equilibrium between reaching enough members of the target group frequently enough. Let's take two extreme examples. One extreme could be to select a medium vehicle the audience of which is fully in the target group, and 10% of the target group is covered. An advertiser might decide to put all her money in ads in this vehicle. That would lead to the lowest possible CPM, and the highest GRP and frequency for the budget. This is not a good media plan: net reach is too low and frequency is unduly high. At the other side of the spectrum, the advertiser may select medium vehicles that all partially cover a different part of the target group, leading to a reach of 70%. However, this would also be a bad media plan. It would lead to low GRP and zero effective reach. The "ideal" plan would be a mixture of both scenarios, a compromise between reach and effective frequency.

Scheduling

With respect to scheduling, advertisers have a number of possibilities. A *continuous schedule* means that the advertiser spends a continuous amount of money per day, week, or month throughout the whole campaign period. In the case of budget constraints, a continuous schedule might result in too low expenditures per period to be effective. Continuous advertising at low levels is also called "*dripping*." This can be meaningful in a philosophy of 360-degree communication to have short but frequent touch points with the target group. A *pulsing schedule* means that a certain level of advertising takes place during the whole campaign period ("dripping"), but during particular periods higher advertising levels are used. A *flighting schedule* is used when advertising is concentrated in only a few periods and not during the whole campaign period. In other words, during some periods no advertising takes place, and high levels are spent during peak months ("waves"). Typically, many campaigns have two waves, a launch wave, and a couple of months later a reminder wave. One last tactic worth mentioning is *double-spotting*: two spots of the same brand (usually a longer and a shorter one) are placed within the same advertising block (on TV or radio) to increase the likelihood of obtaining effective frequency.

Finally, as mentioned before, with respect to online media, the following has to be noticed. Due to the interactive nature of digital media, people can react to digital ads: they can click-through on banners or on native ads on social media, and like and share a comment on social media content. In that respect, in the online environment, often the distinction is made between owned, paid, and earned media. *Owned media* are media that are owned by the advertiser (e.g., an electronic newsletter, Facebook pages, brand communities). *Paid media* are advertisements that are paid for (e.g., a Google AdWords campaign). *Earned media* is exposure to an advertiser's message as a result of brand engagement activities of website visitors (e.g., liking, sharing, commenting upon a branded message), or creating branded user-generating content (e.g., a video featuring the brand). Companies use viral marketing to generate customer engagement and to "earn" media.

Notes

1. *De Morgen*, March 16, 2021; *De Standaard*, April 3, 2021.
2. https://blog.hootsuite.com/instagram-statistics/.
3. https://www.contagious.com/news-and-views/german-rail-campaign -facebook-sheryl-sandberg-called-the-future-of-advertising; http://www.our -work.de/noneedtofly_automation/; https://www.contagious.com/news- and-views/doppelganger-destinations-sell-staycations-to-germans; https://wersm.com/how-deutsche-bahn-increased-sales-by-24-thanks-to -instagram/.
4. https://contagious.com/io/article/insight-and-strategy-nulla-puo-fermarci -stop-at-nothing.

5   Advertising effectiveness

When has an advertising campaign been successful? The answer to that question is easy: when it has reached or surpassed its goals. Measurement of effectiveness thus always has to refer back to the goals that were laid down in the advertising plan. However, measuring the results of a campaign is not obvious. Its effect on sales, market share, or profits can often not be isolated, and the commercial pay-off of advertising is in many cases only visible after a certain period of time. Therefore, in most campaigns "intermediate" goals are set and results are measured accordingly, such as the attitude toward the ad, brand awareness, brand knowledge, attitude, preference or purchase intention, and activation, and they are assumed to be necessary conditions or even predictors of commercial success. There are three basic types of advertising effectiveness research: pre-testing, post-testing, and campaign evaluation research. Following the development of an advertising strategy, a number of advertising tools (print advertisements, television spots, outdoor posters, online ads, etc.) are developed and tested. This process is called pre-testing. After the development of the campaign, it is placed in the media. The impact of each of the tools can be assessed in post-tests. Finally, the results of the whole campaign can be compared with its objectives in campaign evaluation research.

Pre-testing

In a *pre-test*, advertising stimuli are tested before they appear in the media. The general purpose is to test an ad concept, different concepts, or finalized advertising stimuli to assess whether or not they can achieve the purpose for which they are designed. Often, advertising agencies develop different concepts or executions of a new campaign. The first function of pre-testing is to select the most appropriate one. The agency then goes back to the drawing board to "polish" the chosen advertising concept into finalized stimuli. These can then again be pre-tested before media placement. Advertising stimuli should generate a number of intermediate processes or effects, such as creating attention, carrying over information, evoking acceptance of the message, credibility, positive affective reactions about the ad and the brand, activation, and purchase intention. In a pre-test the extent to which these intermediate effects are generated is tested. It is important to understand that pre-tests cannot be used to forecast sales, market shares, or profits. Often, a campaign consists of a number of similar ads, i.e., different executions of the same basic communications strategy. Evidently, not all formats are equally appealing. A pre-test can help in establishing the extent to which some executions are more effective than others in that respect, and assist in deciding upon the optimal frequency of placement of the various ads. However, the latter is not an easy one to pre-test in a valid way. Usually, consumers see ads frequently over some period of time. It is difficult, if not impossible, to mimic this exposure process realistically.

Three basic categories of ad pre-tests can be distinguished: a number of desirable characteristics can be tested internally, and samples of consumers can be used to test communication and behavioral effects of a campaign. A campaign can be tested internally by the advertising agency and/ or the advertiser by means of a checklist or readability analysis. *Pre-test checklists* are used to make sure that nothing important is missing, and that the ad is appealing, powerful, and "on strategy" (i.e., whether it targets the right consumers with the right messages aiming at the right goals, as laid out in the briefing to the agency), the product is shown (in use), and the brand name is mentioned frequently enough. The problem with these checklists is that they are often only judged by insiders, such as brand or advertising managers and agencies. Many of the items in these checklists should in fact be tested with members of the target group of the campaign. Another type of internal test is the *readability analysis.* Good advertising copy is simple and easy to understand "at first glance." Several methods have been developed to test this "readability." For instance, a number of words in the text (e.g., every sixth word) can be removed, and a sample of consumers can be asked to fill in the missing words. The number of correctly reproduced words is an indication of the readability of the text. Research indicates that easy-to-read copy contains short sentences with short, concrete, and familiar words, and lots of personal references.

Communications or activation effects are measured in a sample of customers of the target group. The distinction can be made between physiological or observation tests, recall tests, direct opinion measurement, and behavioral tests.

In a *physiological test* the reaction of the body to advertising stimuli is measured. Two types of physiological measurements can be carried out. The first is measurement of arousal, i.e., the activation of the nervous system, which is an indication of the intensity of the effect evoked by an ad. Several observational experimental techniques are used. For instance, the higher the arousal, the more the pupil of the eye dilates. Pupil dilation measurement is therefore used to assess the amount of arousal during, for instance, a TV commercial. Another measure is the galvanic skin response. In this method, the varying humidity of the skin is measured by means of an electric current, on the basis of which the amount of arousal can be assessed. Most of these techniques are complicated and expensive, while the results are often difficult to interpret. Therefore, they are not frequently used. For an ad to be effective, it has at least to be noted, and a minimum of information has to be carried over. An often used technique in this regard is *eye camera research*: it registers which sections of a stimulus (a print ad, a website, or a TV commercial) are looked at, for how long, how frequently, and in what order. Today, eye camera research takes place by means of laptops on which an eye camera is mounted that registers eye movements of participants in the study sitting in front of the laptop. This technique can be used to improve the structure or layout of an ad. It can also be used to test websites.

In *recall tests*, such as the *portfolio test*, the extent to which an individual recalls a new ad or a new execution amid existing ads is tested. The ad to be tested is put in a portfolio, together with other ads. The subject is asked to look at the ads, and sometime later (20 or 30 minutes), the recall test takes place. The subject has to name the ads and the brands, as well as the content of the ad that he or she can remember. Ads that are more frequently recognized are assumed to have drawn the attention better. Recall tests have a number of limitations. First of all, the more one is interested in a certain product (because one is planning to buy it in the near future, for instance), the more attention is paid to the ad and the better it is recalled. Additionally, very often the recall test is carried out very briefly after the exposure. The subject does not really have time to forget the ad. Ideally, the time between the exposure and the recall test should be as long as the time between the exposure and the buying situation in real life, but this can hardly be organized in a controlled lab experiment like the portfolio test. Results of recall tests, and in fact of any other advertising effectiveness test, should be benchmarked, i.e., compared to relevant alternatives measured in comparable test groups. For instance, the results of a test for a new car ad should be compared with the results of other car ads or different stimuli for the same car campaign. The test of a new car ad should not be carried out in a group of car fanatics and compared to test results of car ads in a group of people who are not so much interested in cars. Often, in this and other types of ad effectiveness tests, the quality of ads is expressed as how high they score compared to other previously tested comparable campaigns, for instance in the top 10% for recall of the brand, the top 15% for recall of the tagline, and so on.

In *direct opinion measurement tests*, a jury of customers is exposed to a number of ads and asked to rate the ads on a number of characteristics. Ad elements that can be tested are clarity, informativeness, novelty, evoked feelings, evoked attitude toward the ad and the brand, interest, quality of the information, the extent to which an ad induces the person to buy the product, and so on. The participants may be asked to rate each ad on a number of scale items, or to order them on the basis of a number of criteria. The most important disadvantage of the direct rating method is that individuals are exposed to ads in a very unnatural environment. Therefore, they may be inclined to approach the ads too rationally compared with a real-life situation of ad exposure. This phenomenon is known as the "consumer jury effect." Also in this test, benchmarking is important.

Finally, behavior pre-tests try to measure actual behavior. In a *trailer test* or *coupon-stimulated purchasing test*, respondents visiting a supermarket are invited to a trailer in a supermarket car park, and randomly assigned to an experimental or a control group. The members of the first group are shown a commercial that is being tested and asked a number of questions. The control group has to answer the same questions without being exposed to the commercial. Several experimental groups can be formed if different commercials have to be tested. Both groups receive a number of coupons as a reward for their cooperation. An individualized store card registers the items purchased. Ad effectiveness is measured by means of differences in redemption between the various coupons. Again, the participants know that they are being tested, and this might influence their buying behavior.

Although pre-testing procedures are very valuable, they have some limitations that should be taken into account when interpreting their results. A pre-test will never lead to the best possible ad, but only to the best ad out of a number of stimuli tested. Pre-testing is only "a guide to better advertising." Pre-testing is only useful when the ads are tested in an individual interviewing procedure. Since ads are processed individually, they should also be tested individually, and not in a group setting in which the influence of the other members of the group invalidates the test rather than being synergetic. Most pre-tests take place in an experimental setting. Consumers may behave differently when exposed to an ad in a real-life situation. Some pre-test methods, such as the direct opinion method, are susceptible to consumer jury effects. Often the effectiveness of the ad is measured almost immediately after exposure. The effect of the elapse of time on ad effectiveness is not assessed. The effect of repetition or frequency of exposure on ad effectiveness cannot easily be assessed. In any case, pre-tests can only provide guidance in terms of intermediate effects of a campaign, such as ad recall or recognition, recalling or understanding the core message, the attitude and feelings toward the ad, the extent to which the ad supports brand image, stimulates activation, or might lead to buying intention. They cannot predict actual sales, market shares, number of new customers, and other "hard" campaign results.

Post-testing

A *post-test* is a test of the effectiveness of a single ad (TV, online banner, radio spot, magazine) after placement in the media. Three types of post-tests can be distinguished: measurement of exposure, communications effect tests, and measurement of behavior. First of all, the extent to which an ad has reached its audience can be measured. Net reach, Gross Rating Points (GRP), Opportunity to See (OTS), and other exposure measures can be calculated (see Chapter 4). In measuring the communications or message processing effects of an ad, two types of tests are used: recognition and recall tests. A *recognition test* is a test in which a sample of ads is presented to a consumer, who is asked to indicate whether he or she recognizes the ad or not. The underlying assumption is that ads can only be effective when they are at least noted and processed. A well-known recognition test procedure for print ads is the *Starch test*. Consumers who say they have read a specific issue in a magazine or a newspaper are interviewed. The magazine is opened at a random page, and a number of questions are asked per ad. The procedure leads to four percentage scores for each ad:

- *Non-readers*: the percentage of people who do not remember having seen the ad.
- *Noted*: the percentage of readers who claim to have seen the ad.
- *Seen/associated*: the percentage of readers who claim to have read the product and brand name.
- *Read most*: the percentage of readers who claim to have read at least half the ad.

Obviously, the Starch test is very susceptible to the test subject's honesty.

In a *masked identification test*, part of an ad, usually the brand name, is covered. The subject is asked if he or she recognizes the ad, and if he or she knows what brand it is for. Recognition and correct attribution scores of the brand to the ad can then be calculated. Brand confusion (attributing a wrong brand to an advertisement) can be measured too. The combination of recognition and correct attribution scores leads to the *useful score*: the percentage of the test sample that both recognized the ad and attributed it correctly to the brand advertised. An example of the results of a masked identification test of a billboard campaign for a new car is shown in Figure 5.1, together with the results of a number of categories of control ads. Here again, benchmarking is important: the effectiveness of an advertising stimulus can only be assessed based on comparisons with other similar ads. "Similar" can be ads for the same product category, or ads during the same period, or ads in the same medium. In this example, the two waves of billboard advertising for the new car show recognition scores of 90% and 80%, a lot more than the 50% for all advertising campaigns, 60% for 20 m^2 billboards (the same format of the car campaign) and 55% for all car billboards. Correct attribution of the first new car wave is 70%, and a lower 55% for the second wave, larger than the 40–50% attribution of the control categories. Consequently, the useful score of the two new car waves is much higher (56% and 44%) than that of the control categories (20–27.5%). Masked identification tests can also be used to measure if the target audience can attribute the tagline or main message of an advertising stimulus, for instance by covering this tagline or message instead of the brand name.

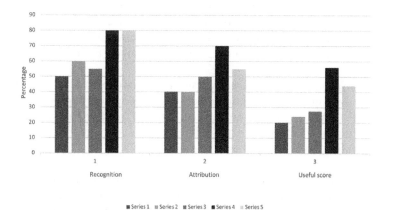

Series 1: All ads   Series 2: All 20 m² ads   Series 3: All car ads
Series 4: 20 m² brand X first wave   Series 5: 20 m² brand X second wave

Figure 5.1   Masked identification test

A second type of communications effect measurement is the *recall test*. In an unaided recall test, consumers have to indicate which ads they remember having seen, in a specific magazine, on TV, websites, or billboards. In an aided recall test, the consumer's memory is helped by means of clues such as: What car ads did you see on TV yesterday? Unaided recall scores are usually lower than aided recall scores, which in turn are lower than recognition scores. Therefore they cannot be compared. A well-known recall test is the *Gallup–Robinson Impact test* for print ads. Firstly, the respondents have to read a magazine at home. The following day, the respondents are called and asked to recall as many ads as they can. After that, a number of questions about the content of the ads are asked. The Gallup–Robinson procedure leads to three indicators of advertising effectiveness:

- *Proved name registration*: the percentage of subjects who remember an ad without having seen it during the test.
- *Idea penetration*: the percentage of subjects who have understood the main idea in the ad.

- *Conviction*: the percentage of subjects who want to buy or use the product.

Most post-test are conducted via personal or online surveys and measure similar indicators: recognition, attribution (+ useful score), and several quality perception attributes, such as clarity, convincingness, credibility, likeability, originality, and how pleasant or annoying the ads are.

Finally, the effect of an ad can be tested by means of behavioral measures. Especially in the case of direct response ads, the number of people calling a free telephone number announced in the ad, sending back a coupon, clicking on a weblink, or actually buying the product can be considered a measure of the effectiveness of the ad.

Recall and recognition tests have a number of limitations. In recognition tests, consumers can say what they like; they can lie, exaggerate, or guess. An ad that is part of a campaign of similar ads will be more easily recognized or recalled. In integrated campaigns that use various media, it is hard to isolate the effect of one single ad. Recognizing or recalling advertising may be a necessary condition to buy a product, but often not a sufficient one. Product involvement influences the results of the test. A consumer who is very interested in a certain product category will perform better in recognizing ads for this product category. This does not imply anything about the effectiveness of that specific ad. Recall is, in a number of cases, an irrelevant indication of advertising effectiveness. The only thing recall tests measure is whether the ad has been able to draw attention. Finally, recall scores are very dependent on the time elapsed between exposure and recall measurement.

A specific post-testing format for online ads is the *A/B test*, also known as the split test. *A/B testing* is a real-time real-live experiment to find out to what extent two or more variations of an online advertisement perform better by presenting each version to groups of users at random at the same time, and analyzing the results to determine which variation performs better for a given advertising goal (conversion, sales …). A/B testing demonstrates the efficacy of online advertising stimuli, based on behavioral effects data. Based on A/B tests, an advertiser can withdraw specific stimuli (banners, native ads) that are not or less effective, replace stimuli with other ones, or adapt stimuli, all in real time. This allows for short-term optimization of an advertising campaign at minimal cost. Elements of an ad that can be A/B tested include the headline or subject line, imagery, CTA forms and language, layout, fonts, and colors. It is crucial to only run one test at a time, i.e., to pick one variable to test, for instance, the number of viewers who subscribe to an e-newsletter after clicking on a link in a native ad, or make a purchase after exposure to the ad. Testing one change at a time will show which affected users' behavior and which did not. To prove causality, an A/B test needs controls, the elements that are kept the same throughout the experiment. One variable to control for is time, i.e., the period during which the test is run. The period for an A/B test must be the same for both "A" and "B" variables so that the user base seeing each version is the same. Further, substantially different "competing" advertising stimuli should be selected to do the test, and ideally sufficiently large subsamples of viewers should be selected that are equally and randomly exposed to one of the test ads. But even relatively small sample sizes can provide significant, actionable results as to which changes are most engaging for users. A/B testing and adapting campaign stimuli accordingly will ideally make the adapted final versions of the advertising stimuli better, and will help to keep visitors on site longer, more quickly click through, or convert. Determining a winner and a loser of an A/B test is straightforward: which stimulus metrics come closer to its goals (time spent, conversions, etc.). Further, A/B testing can also provide inspiration to apply them in subsequent campaigns.

Campaign evaluation research

Campaign evaluation research focuses on the effectiveness of a whole advertising campaign on brand parameters. As in post-tests, a before or control measurement is necessary to assess adequately the effect of a particular campaign. Communications as well as behavior effects can be measured. Communications effects measurements can be structured following the HoE logic and be measured by means of surveys with samples of the target groups: awareness, knowledge, attitude, and intention to buy. *Top-of-mind awareness* (TOMA) measurement is an unaided awareness test in which the consumer is asked which brand of a specific product category is the first one that comes to mind. Subsequently, the consumer is asked if he or she can name other brands in the same product category (*unaided awareness*). Finally, a number of brands are mentioned, and the consumer has to indicate the ones he or she knows (*aided awareness*). The advertising campaign is not mentioned but, by comparing the awareness before and after a campaign, its effect on brand awareness can be assessed. Furthermore, brand awareness rates of competitive products are also measured, and can serve as a control measurement or benchmark. Often a campaign aims at changing the target group's opinion about certain aspects or attributes of a brand. Measurement scales can be used to measure this change in attitude or image components. Finally, the communications effect of a campaign can be measured on the basis of a target group of consumers' intention to buy: "The next time you buy coffee, what is the chance that you will buy brand X (as a percentage, or on a 10-point scale)?" An alternative measure is the *Net Promoter Score* (NPS), which is based on the question: "To which degree would you recommend the following brand to your family or friends?" measured on a 0–10-point scale. Customers that answer 9 or 10 are called "promoters"; those answering 7 or 8 are "passives"; and those who answer 0–6 are "distractors." The net promoter score is then calculated by subtracting the percentage of people scoring 0–6 from the percentage of people who scored 8–10. NPS can thus take values between −100 and +100. Obviously, NPS scores should be benchmarked, i.e., compared with previous scores and/or with scores of competing brands or companies. NPS can be a good indicator of customer loyalty, provided the industry consists of enough players and customers have a real choice, and customers can easily switch from one supplier to another. On the other hand, NPS is too simple. It does not say how results can be improved, and it is focused on existing customers and not on new ones. It also does not give any information about competitors: they can win a lot of new customers by attracting passives or detractors from other companies. Passives are not taken into account. However, they are indeed also "not satisfied" customers that can be seduced to switch to competitors.

Besides intention to buy and to recommend, the effectiveness of an advertising campaign can also be measured by means of *activation measures*. They measure the extent to which people actively react to advertising by, for instance, looking up further information, talking to friends (buzz), visit a website, or going to a store. Online activation can be measured by means of tracking people's behavior when exposed to a campaign; for instance, click on a link, leave an email address on a landing page, subscribe to a newsletter, request an e-book, download an infographic, or order a trial sample of the product.

As in all before/after measurements, problems of interpretation arise. The effect of a campaign cannot always be isolated. A deteriorating image, for instance, may be the result of, among others, a bad campaign, a price increase, bad publicity, competitors' actions, an inappropriate sales promotion campaign, or a bad distribution strategy. Furthermore, the effect of advertising campaigns may only become visible after some time. The performance of a brand immediately after the campaign may therefore underestimate its true impact in the long run.

Obviously, the ultimate objective of an advertising campaign is to make people buy the product, become loyal, and eventually to make a (better) profit. In behavior tests the relation between advertising and buying behavior is studied directly. Various behavioral measures of ad effectiveness can be distinguished, the most obvious ones being sales and market share evolution. Again, as in all campaign evaluation measurements, it should be noted that the evolution of market share and sales may be attributable to other marketing mix instruments than advertising. The effect of an advertising campaign cannot always be isolated easily. Apart from changes in sales, more specific behavioral effects can be measured, such as trial purchases and the degree of adoption of, or loyalty to, a brand. An analysis combining awareness and behavioral measures to assess the effectiveness of advertising campaigns is the *awareness–trial–retention framework*. Three indicators are measured by means of surveys with the target groups at various moments in time:

- *Awareness rate*: number of target group members that are aware of the brand/number of people in the target group.
- *Trial rate*: number of target group members that have purchased the brand at least once during a given period/number of target group members that are aware of the brand.
- *Retention rate*: number of people that have purchased the brand at least a specific number of times during the same period/number of target group members that have purchased the brand at least once during a given period.

Evidently, the period under study and the number of times a consumer has to have purchased the product to be called a loyal consumer have to be determined in advance, and will depend upon the product category studied. Suppose that for two competing brands the results in Table 5.1 have been obtained after an advertising campaign.

Table 5.1   Awareness, trial, and retention rates for two
hypothetical brands

	Brand A	Brand B
Awareness rate	70%	20%
Trial rate	40%	20%
Retention rate	10%	70%

The end result is the same for both brands: 2.8% of the target group has become loyal to the brand (70 x 40 x 10 = 20 x 20 x 70). However, the three indicators show a more differentiated picture. Brand B was not very successful in building awareness and trial. One might say that the advertising campaign was not very effective. On the other hand, the marketing strategy seems to be on target: most people who have tried the product have become loyal to it. Brand A has had a successful advertising campaign, but something seems to be wrong with the rest of the marketing strategy (low retention rate). Maybe the product is of bad quality, the price too high, or the distribution strategy inappropriate. It could also be that the product is a luxury item, for which in the short run trial is more important than repeat purchase.

Measuring online advertising effectiveness

The purpose of online advertising is in many ways the same as that of traditional ads and, consequently, the effectiveness of online campaigns can be measured by means of the same indicators. However, a particular characteristic of the Internet is that all information about site traffic can be tracked. Analyzing these files is one way of tracking website performance and social media advertising campaigns. The results of online advertising campaigns are more measurable than those of campaigns in traditional offline media.

The most basic method to measure brand website effectiveness is by asking for feedback on the website to find out who really visits a website and what their evaluation of site, the brand, and sales effects are, by means of visitor surveys (online or offline). This can be done by asking visitors to leave a contact email address or by inserting a feedback form on one of the web pages. Surveys may give socio-demographic, psychographic, and webographic (Internet use data) profiles of visitors. They can also measure attitudes, satisfaction, and intentions. In pre-testing, usability testing and post-testing of websites, qualitative market research techniques such as focus groups and in-depth interviewing can be used in conjunction with quantitative Internet panel surveys to add research insights to website visitor surveys. As to social media campaigns, advertisers need to know upfront what their qualitative and quantitative goals are before they can measure how successful their efforts have been in achieving them: e.g., driving more traffic to the website, increasing the fan base, reaching specific target groups, increasing brand awareness or brand activation, selling more products, getting more positive reviews, establishing the brand or company as a leader. Just as in any other effectiveness measurement context, benchmarks should be used, such as past traffic, sales figures, review counts, fan base, page visits, and so on.

There are several categories of metrics to assess social media advertising performance. One framework distinguishes three categories:

- *Activity metrics* measure the activity of the company on social media: number, frequency and recency of updates, reactions, photos and videos posted, the creativity of the content, etc.
- *Interaction metrics* measure to what extent target audiences engage with content: number, frequency and recency of reactions, tags, mentions, likes, shares, favorites, links, downloads, friends, followers, fans, shared updates, reviews, website visits, sentiment (the valence of the reactions), recommendations, etc. These indicators are called *brand engagement measures*. Three basic types of brand engagement can be distinguished: *Consumption* (e.g., brand pages visited or looking at advertisements), *Contribution* (e.g., liking, sharing, and making comments on brand communication), and *Creation* (producing user-generated content as a result of being exposed to brand communication, e.g., posting a video).
- *Performance metrics* reveal to what extent social media activity has contributed directly or indirectly to a company's business results. These measures indicate costs and return of online activity (return on investment), such as shifts in the attitude towards the brand, satisfaction, perceptions, sales, market share, and profit. Commonly used performance metrics that provide an indication of campaign

cost efficiency are the CPM (views of an ad), CPC (someone clicking through to the landing page of the campaign), and CPA (someone doing something you intended him to do, such as leaving an email address, becoming a lead, or making a sale).

Another social media metrics framework distinguishes four categories of effectiveness measures (all but the last one measured relative to the number of viewers, i.e., the number of people exposed to the post):

- *Conversation rate*: the number of responses to a post.
- *Applause rate*: the number of times anyone shows positive appreciation of a social media post (likes, favorites).
- *Amplification rate*: the number of times an update or a post is shared, retweeted, etc.
- *Economic value*: the total short- and long-term return and cost savings of social media activity.

Table 5.2 provides an overview of specific metrics that are often used in tracking online advertising and e-commerce effectiveness. All social media provide a number of these metrics, variants thereof, or metrics that are specific for the platform, to track the effectiveness of social media advertising campaigns. For instance, on Facebook, besides impressions, click-throughs and conversions, the number of likes, shares, and comments can also be tracked. On Twitter, the number of comments, responses, and retweets, the ratio of negative to positive tweets, and the number of followers can be monitored. Similar metrics are available on Pinterest and Snapchat. On mobile, advertisers can, for instance, keep track of visits to a physical store, check maps for directions, requests for more information, SMSs and notifications to friends, and share locations or offers with friends.

Plenty of tools are available to measure brand website performance and the results of social media advertising efforts. Most social media platforms provide their own tools to manage a campaign and to track its effectiveness with respect to different metrics. Most advertisers use *data management platforms* (DMPs) to track the effectiveness of their campaigns. A DMP is a platform to collect, organize, and activate data from any source, including online, offline, and mobile. It is the backbone of data-driven marketing and allows businesses to gain unique insights into their customers. One of the best known DMPs is Google Analytics (Box 5.1). It allows brand and advertising managers to gain insights into

Table 5.2   Online advertising and e-commerce tracking measures

Ad display metrics and web shop performance	
Impressions	Number of times an ad is seen
Click-through rate (CTR)	Percentage of times an ad is clicked by those who have seen it
View-through rate (VTR)	Percentage of times an ad is not clicked immediately, but the website is visited within 30 days
Hits	Number of web visits
Page views	Number of pages viewed on a website
Viewability rate	Share of ads that are actually seen online
Unique visitors	Number of unique visitors of a website in each period
Loyalty	Measured in different ways, e.g., number of page views, frequency of single-use visits to the website, percentage of customers who return to the site in a year to make additional purchases
Reach	Number of website visitors who are potential buyers, or the percentage of total buyers who buy at a site
Recency	Time elapsed since the last action undertaken by a buyer, such as a website visit or purchase
Stickiness (duration)	Average length of stay at a website
Acquisition rate	Percentage of visitors who indicate an interest in the website's products by registering or visiting product pages
Conversion rate	Percentage of visitors who become customers
Browse-to-buy ratio	Ratio of items purchased to product views
View-to-cart ratio	Ratio of "add to cart" clicks to product views
Cart conversion rate	Ratio of actual orders to "add to cart" clicks
Checkout conversion rate	Ratio of actual orders to checkouts started
Abandonment rate	Percentage of shoppers who begin a shopping cart purchase but then leave the website without completing a purchase
Retention rate	Percentage of existing customers who continue to buy on a regular basis (like "loyalty")
Attrition rate	Percentage of customers who do not return during the next year after an initial purchase

Video advertising metrics	
View time	The time an ad stays in view while it plays
Completion rate	How many viewers watch the complete video as a percentage of those who were exposed to it
Skip rate	How many viewers skipped the video as a percentage of those who were exposed to it
Email metrics	
Delivery rate	Percentage of email recipients who received the mail
Open rate	Percentage of email recipients who open the email and are exposed to the message
Click-through rate	Percentage of recipients who clicked through to offers
Bounce-back rate	Percentage of emails that could not be delivered
Unsubscribe rate	Percentage of recipients who click "unsubscribe"
Conversion rate	Percentage of recipients who actually buy

Source: K.C. Laudon and C.G. Traver (2019), *E-commerce 2018: Business, Technology, Society*, Pearson.

how many (unique) visitors their site has per day/week/month/etc., how visitors use their site, how they arrived on the site (from which site, using which search terms, etc.), from which countries, and so on. Content reports give insights into which parts of the website are performing well, which pages are most popular, and how much time the surfer is spending on these pages, in order to create a better experience for the visitor, prospect, or customer. Social media (what visitors are sharing and where) and mobile (know which mobile platforms work best, see where mobile traffic comes from) are also incorporated. Conversion parameters give insights into the number of customers that the brand or the company attracts, how much it sells, and how users are engaging with the site. Google Analytics can also be used for analyzing an online advertising campaign. All digital channels such as search, display, social, affiliate, and email can be included to see the effect on conversion rates and return. Other DMPs (e.g., Socialbakers) give insights into the kind of attention that posts and updates are getting. It also shows the reach, sentiment, and passion that followers have for a name or brand. It also gives insights into the key terms that are typically associated with a brand. DMP Buffer helps users collaborate, plan, and publish content that drives meaningful engagement and brand growth across platforms like Facebook, Twitter, Pinterest, and

LinkedIn from one dashboard. Brandwatch allows users to manage brand conversations online, create relevant and personalized content, analyze performance against competitors, and take crisis management action.

Box 5.1   Practice: tracking website visits with Google Analytics

This Google Analytics example gives an overview of the visits to the website of a course program at the University of Antwerp and compares the first three months of 2020 (old website) and 2021 (new website). The number of visits per day is shown for both periods in Figure 5.2. Results are shown per channel (traffic source), i.e., how visitors reached the website (rows) in Table 5.3. *Organic* is traffic from search engine results that is earned, not via paid ads (people clicking on a link after entering a key word in Google). *Direct* is any traffic where the referrer or source is unknown, mostly visitors who went directly to the site. *Referral* is traffic that occurs when a user finds the website through a site other than a major search engine. *Paid search* is traffic from search engine results that is the result of paid advertising via Google AdWords or another paid search platform (i.e., clicking on the ad). *Social* is traffic from a social network, such as Facebook, LinkedIn, Twitter, or Instagram. *Other* is traffic that does not fit into another source, for instance a paid ad on social media.[1]

Per channel, and for both periods, the number of visits (called "sessions"), the average viewing time per session, the bounce rate (the percentage of people who have only visited one page of the website), and the target conversion ratio is given. The latter is the overall percentage of visits that resulted in one of the target conversions, such as registration for "open days," information days, or "keep me informed," downloading brochures, leaving contact details, or staying on the website for more than three minutes. The "relative importance" column shows the percentage of visits for each channel. Visits from UAntwerp student and staff were removed from the data. Compared to the first quarter of 2020, in the first quarter of 2021, the number of sessions and the target conversion ratio have increased, and the bounce rate decreased (which is good). However, the average time visitors stayed on the website dropped.

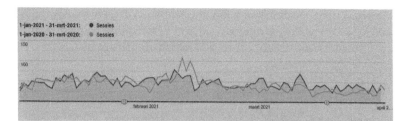

Figure 5.2   Traffic (number of visits) to a course program section of the University of Antwerp website, first quarter 2020 and 2021

Table 5.3   Google Analytics output for a course program website performance

Channel	Period	Relative importance (%)	Sessions	Average duration	Bounce ratio (%)	Target convers- ion ratio (%)
All channels	2020	–	4451	2:42	45.39	23.80
	2021	–	2045	3:10	50.00	19.50
			+117.65%	-14.51%	-9.23	+22.50
Organic	2020	89.10	3966	2:39	44.56	22.01
	2021	82.93	1696	3:37	43.40	18.40
			+133.84%	-26.67%	+2.90	+19.66
Direct	2020	7.28	324	2:17	57.72	34.57
	2021	14.03	287	0:04	86.76	4.18
			+12.89%	+3297.36%	-33.48	+726.75
Referral	2020	1.95	87	8:32	28.74	13.79
	2021	0	0	0	0	0
Paid	2020	1.12	50	0:53	50.00	100.00
	2021	3.03	62	5:17	59.68	100.00
			-19.35%	-83.17%	-16.22	
Social	2020	0.27	12	1:00	0	0
	2021	0	0	0	0	0
Other	2020	0.27	12	0	100.00	100.00
	2021	0	0	0	0	0

Note: 2020 and 2021 refer to the first three months of each year.

Note

1.   https://www.smartbugmedia.com/blog/what-is-the-difference-between
     -direct-and-organic-search-traffic-sources.

6   Advertising ethics

Morals are beliefs that individuals hold concerning what is right or wrong. Morals direct people as they make decisions. *Ethics* are operational guidelines for both individuals and organizations. They are in fact "applied morals," those practices and activities that are importantly right or wrong.

Different views can be held on how to apply ethical decision-making in marketing (communications). Under the *caveat emptor* rule, anything is allowed that maximizes profits within the law: what is legal must therefore also be ethical. The *ethics code* view strives for standards guidelines that go further than the law on the basis of which companies' and industries' ethical performance is judged, or at least to which they aspire. In the *consumer sovereignty* approach, ethical marketing decisions are determined by the answer to three important questions: Is the target market vulnerable in ways that limit consumer decision-making (consumer capability) and are consumers' expectations at purchase likely to be realized; do consumers have sufficient information to judge (consumer information) and can consumers go elsewhere; would they incur substantial costs or inconvenience by transferring their loyalty (consumer choice)? Finally, there is the *caveat venditor* principle, which implies that the maximization of consumer satisfaction or well-being should be the ultimate aim of marketing action.

Others hold that any advertising decision should in any case be legal, decent, honest, and truthful. *Legal* means that it should be allowed under the current regulations and laws of the country in which the company operates. *Decent* means that it should not contain anything that is likely to cause widespread offence, fear, or distress; for instance, the use of shocking claims or images for the sake of creating attention should be avoided, unless a valid and acceptable reason is given. *Honest and truthful* implies that it should not exploit inexperience or lack of knowledge of consumers; no claims should be made which are inaccurate, ambiguous, or intended to mislead, whether through explicit statement or through omission. A distinction can be made between *deceptive advertising* and unfair practices. Consumers are deceived when there is a claim–fact discrepancy and the false claim is believed by customers. Moreover, the message must be misleading (i.e., representation, omission, or practice that is likely to mislead the customer) from the perspective of a reasonable consumer (i.e., by a reasonable number of the group to which the practice is targeted), and the deceptive practice must be material (i.e., important and likely to impact on consumers' choice or conduct regarding the product and thus relate to a central characteristic). *Unfair advertising* are acts or practices that cause or are likely to cause substantial harm to consumers, which are not reasonably avoidable by consumers themselves, and not outweighed by countervailing benefits to consumers or competitors, e.g., advertising that offends public policy as it has been established by statutes, is immoral, unethical, oppressive, or unscrupulous, or causes substantial injury to consumers, competitors, or other businesses.

Ethical issues in advertising

Ethical issues in advertising originate from the clash between business practice and social concerns, such as environmental and social values and societal notions about honesty, honor, virtue, and integrity. Marketing and marketing communications have often been accused of many allegedly unethical practices and consequences, such as creating a materialistic culture of conspicuous consumption, playing on emotions, simplifying real human situations into stereotypes, exploiting anxieties, employing techniques of intensive persuasion that amount to (hidden) manipulation, maximizing appeal and minimizing information, trivializing, generally reducing men, women, and children to the role of irrational consumer, and invading people's privacy. Of all the marketing communications instruments, advertising is the one that receives most criticism because of its alleged untruthful, deceptive, and manipulative nature; offensive and in bad taste formats; and because it makes people buy things they do not really need and compromises people's autonomy. On the other hand, persuasion is a legitimate form of human interaction and, as such, there is nothing inherently unethical in trying to persuade a person to buy a product or a service. Nevertheless, there are countless advertising practices that are (heavily) criticized. The loudest criticisms relate to misleading the consumer, perpetuating stereotypes, using controversial shock tactics, covert tactics, inappropriately targeting vulnerable groups, particularly children, and invading privacy. Additionally, a number of industries are particularly vulnerable to unethical practices.

Deception

Advertising is expected not to be *deceptive or misleading*, by misusing or omitting information on material facts (for instance, the health side effects of medication), statistics, or research. A special category of potentially misleading advertising is *puffery*, the use of hyperbole or exaggeration of claims to promote a brand. Puffery is sometimes called "soft-core deception." On the other hand, puffery may be seen as a legitimate creative technique that is not misleading because any "reasonable" consumer with sufficient cognitive skill knows what is going on. Indeed, traditionally, the ethicality of advertising rests upon the *"reasonable person standard."* It is generally assumed that an ad cannot be considered to be ethically wrong if a "reasonable person" comprehends it correctly. Additionally, the distinction should be made between miscomprehension and deliberate deception. The former is a problem of the consumer (and maybe partly the responsibility of the advertiser), but is not per se an ethical problem. Some ads are indeed unintentionally misleading in the sense that they lead to false beliefs and material harm. However, in those cases, advertising is just miscomprehended. But who is a "reasonable" consumer? And what are "sufficient cognitive skills?" Should not advertisers and governments strive to also appropriately inform and protect less reasonable and less advertising literate consumers?

One specific form of deception is *greenwashing*. Consumers are increasingly sensitive to the sustainability of economic activity and consumption and scrutinize companies in this respect. Advertisers can serve to emphasize the credentials of the sustainable features and benefits of its offerings and to create a positive image regarding environmentally friendly practices. However, some businesses that would like to benefit from these growing needs are not really addressing environmental issues as expected, but would like to take the credit for doing so. This is the practice of greenwashing: making something appear more environmentally friendly than it is in reality, or making it appear environmentally friendly when it is not, with the aim of misleading or deceiving customers. Companies can, for instance, use vague ("natural") or false claims, claims without proof, or false labels.

Stereotyping and idealized portrayal

Stereotyping is an automatic perceptual bias enabling people to construct simplified images of reality. Advertising practitioners make use of stereotyping to quickly transfer the essential meaning of their messages. The elderly are often depicted as ignorant and helpless, and other cultures and/or ethnic groups are often portrayed in a stereotypical way that may offend them and stimulate prejudices in society. One of the most frequently used stereotypes in advertising is *gender stereotyping*. Gender refers to the personal appearance, personality attributes, and socio-sexual roles that society understands to be "masculine" or "feminine". Gender role stereotypes are beliefs that certain psychological and behavioral traits differentiate women and men. From an advertising perspective, gender is an important segmentation variable and oftentimes the basis for developing different marketing strategies that address the particular needs of either gender. Using gender roles can increase advertising performance, such as better brand evaluations and sales. However, from a societal perspective, the stereotypical depiction of men and women in advertising can be problematic, as the way men and women are represented in advertising can create or reinforce unwanted stereotypes. Advertising has often been accused of perpetuating these stereotypes, and of proclaiming and supporting conservative gender roles in society. Through the mechanism of vicarious learning, viewers may adopt potentially stereotypical information about appropriate and socially desirable behavior.

In research, gender role stereotypes are measured by looking at the occupations (working roles, occupational types), nonworking activities (family vs. recreational vs. decorative and relationships with others), and product categories advertised by men and women. Several studies show that women compared to men are more likely to be presented as product users (vs. authority); they are more likely to be presented in a dependent (vs. autonomous) role; and are more often associated with domestic products (body, home, food). They are more often younger; and are more likely presented at home (vs. at work) than men. The largest difference between men and women appears in categories referring to occupational status (e.g., role and location), which suggests that stereotyping is disadvantaging women against men (Box 6.1).

Box 6.1 Research: gender role stereotypes in Belgian TV advertising

A Belgian study set out to see whether gender role depiction in Belgian TV advertising had evolved over time. From a database containing all televised ads broadcast on Belgian commercial TV, commercials from January 2002 to April 2003 and from January 2009 to April 2010 were randomly selected; 250 commercials from the first period and 243 from the second period were selected, in which a total of 907 main characters were portrayed. Both men (50%) and especially women (71%) were mostly presented as young and least in the older age category (11% of men, 8% of woman). Men (39%) appeared more frequently as middle-aged than women (21%). Women (19%) were depicted significantly more often as using a product than men (11%). Women (20%) were significantly more frequently depicted as sexual objects than men (5%). Almost half (44%) of the women in the ads were shown in a domestic setting, while this occurred significantly less frequently for men (30%). Men (27%), by contrast, were proportionally more frequently portrayed in a professional context than women (9%). Within the workplace, the majority of men (55%) are shown as interpreting a superior role, while women are most often shown in a subordinate role (57%). Women (17%) are also more often depicted in a parental role than men (11%). Only 1% of the men in the ads are performing household chores, while this percentage is significantly higher for women (12%). When women are shown in a family context, they are vastly portrayed as dominant within the family (90%), while this is only the case for 25% of the men shown in a family context. Almost all (99%) women and the majority of men (66%) were rated as "not muscular." Men were significantly more often "slightly muscular" (27%) or "strongly muscular" (5%) than women. While 89% of women in the ads were judged to be underweight (vs. 27% of men), men were most likely to be shown in a "normal" weight class (66% vs. 9% of women). Overweight men (5%) and women (2%) were rare.

The study demonstrates that advertising on Belgian TV is permeated by gender stereotypes. Notwithstanding societal and regulatory changes, advertisers keep on using stereotypical gender roles to convey their messages, and there was little decrease from 2002 to 2010.

The use of models in advertising often supports the stereotype that happiness depends on physical attractiveness. Advertising often uses images of unattainable idealizations. The ideal woman is pictured as thin, and the ideal man as buff, and everyone is beautiful. The more these unrealistic and unattainable images are seen, the more people will perceive them as reflecting reality. Social comparison theory posits that individuals compare themselves to others in order to achieve social acceptance and that people may feel inferior if the person or group they are using for comparison is seen as being "better" than themselves. All this leads to the perception of an individual as a physical object viewed by others, increasing the perception of the need to present as positive a physical appearance as possible, and to perceived pressure to conform to these ideal images. As a result, idealized advertising can negatively affect how individuals think about themselves and on their mood and bodily perceptions, leading to unhealthy dieting, body dissatisfaction, and a range of psychological problems including depression and eating disorders. Models being Photoshopped to make them look more "ideal" than they are is a common practice in advertising. This type of advertising is deceptive and violates the autonomy of those subjected to it. On the bright side, advertisements that stress female empowerment (also termed "*femvertising*") have also appeared in recent years. Femvertising challenges and rejects traditional stereotypical images in favor of personal freedom.

A particular form of stereotyping pertains to the stereotypical portrayal and (mis)use of the LGBTQ community, especially gay men. This representation is frequently criticized as stereotypical or even derogative. Today, overt gay and lesbian imagery appears regularly in mainstream advertising, especially of gay men and for brands and in product categories which are associated with edgy and unconventional imagery, such as travel, design, fashion, and alcohol. The (mis)use of the LGBTQ community as a progressive "anchor point" is referred to as *pinkwashing* or *rainbowwashing*. Moreover, the overwhelming majority of represented gay characters in advertising are white, middle-class, gender-normative, and mostly male, otherwise described as "youthful, shirtless, hairless, and muscular." For LGBTQ people, the desire to be portrayed as "normal," that is to say part of the fabric of society and not reduced to simple stereotypes, is important: different facets of diverse personalities should be represented, rather than a reductionist portrayal focusing on sexual orientation alone.

One particular form of ethically questionable stereotyping is *cultural appropriation*, often of indigenous minority groups' culture, defined as the marketing of misappropriated "indigenousness." It appears in branding to advertising to paraphernalia such as clothing: Jeep Cherokee, Chief Crazy Horse liquor. Much of the imagery, brand names, or "sham rituals," such as war chants, misrepresent indigenous communities as primitive savages with blatant racism. Consequently, many consider the use of indigenous people's cultural traditions, symbols, and folklore as offensive or inappropriate. Appropriation takes many forms: non-indigenous people that want to learn indigenous traditional spirituality then turn it into a business (e.g., sweat lodge ceremonies); movies and books adopting real or imagined indigenous traditions (e.g., the movie *Dances with Wolves*); paintings, jewelry, or pottery using indigenous symbols; or the natural health industry that adopts a multitude of healing philosophies from Chinese traditional medicine. In short, indigenous culture can become a commodity that is advertised, exploited, and sold in the marketplace.

Shock advertising

Controversial or "*shock advertising*" is advertising that deliberately startles and offends its audience, by means of norm violation – transgression of law or custom (obscenity) or moral/social code (vulgarity) – or by showing things that outrage the moral or physical senses (e.g., provocative or disgusting images). Controversial advertising appeals and shock tactics are widely used as a creative technique to grab the attention of the target group by means of breaking through the clutter (Box 6.2). Controversial advertising can be divided into two broad categories: advertising for controversial products or ideas (e.g., politics, female hygiene products in some cultures, tobacco, and alcohol; some may even say professional services like dentists, lawyers, and doctors), and controversial imagery, because it is perceived as indecent or causing offence (e.g., indecent language, nudity, sexually oriented, gross depiction, racist, too personal). Several well-known brands are known to have used controversial appeals, the most frequently cited being Benetton, but also Calvin Klein, Citroën, Moschino, Esprit, Gucci, Sony PlayStation, and Reebok. Shock appeals are sometimes used in public service announcements, for instance AIDS awareness campaigns, in which case they can generate a lot of attention to and memory of the message.

Box 6.2 Practice: Suitsupply: is sex the best way to sell suits?

Shock advertising for fashion is not a new phenomenon. Explicit fashion ads started in 1980, when Calvin Klein marketed its jeans using the then 15-year-old Brooke Shields in an attempt to rely on controversial advertising to reach a wider consumer audience. In early 2021, an ad for the men's fashion brand Suitsupply, featuring models in an orgy setting, kissing open-mouthed with tongues, has created anger online. The tagline of the ad "The new normal is coming" refers to the end of the Covid-19 pandemic and the bacchanalian promise of a post-Covid era. The company's CEO and founder defends the ad by stating that post-pandemic life is on the horizon, social distancing for extraordinary long periods of time has conditioned us to fear the proximity of others, and that the campaign was simply a positive outlook on our future where people can get back to gathering and getting close. The physical proximity of the models in the advert is part of a broader trend, with brands such as Diesel and Paco Rabanne all using images recently of couples in passionate scenes.

The campaign and the resulting online buzz seem to have worked: searches for the brand increased by 41% in the week after the advert was launched online. Some say that this is (also) due to the social component to these ads at a time when people long for human touch. One progressive aspect of the latest adverts is that they also feature same-sex couplings. Showing something provocative, like an orgy, helps build buzz among consumers at a time when sales of suits have declined sharply. When many are still social distancing and trying to keep their germs to themselves, an orgy is all the more shocking. That shock can translate into brand awareness.

A particular form of shock tactics are threat-based ads, commonly known as "fear appeals," messages aimed at scaring people to take a certain action (see also Chapter 2). They are often used in social marketing campaigns (don't drink and drive, don't smoke, have safe sex, etc.). Some state that any deliberate fostering of anxiety by advertising is unethical because, like any other ad that exerts emotional pressure, fear appeals can be regarded as manipulative. Further, fear appeals expose a person against his or her will to harmful or seriously offensive images. Moreover, fear may induce reactance, defensive avoidance, and fatalism, and may lead to maladaptive social responses, for instance heightened anxiety among those most at risk and complacency among those not directly targeted.

Covert marketing

Covert marketing is a firm's marketing actions whereby consumers believe that the activities are not those of the firm. It exists in many forms, such as stealth marketing, brand placement, native advertising, buzz marketing, and influencer marketing (see Chapter 2). Some claim that brand placement is the ultimate example of unethical, inherently deceptive advertising, since it is both disguised and obtrusive. Often viewers are not aware of the fact that brands are intentionally placed in TV programs or movies, and they often do not pay conscious attention to them. Therefore, there is a need to protect consumers from being misled. Brand placement or native advertising and influencer marketing *disclosure*, i.e., communicating to the viewers or readers that brands are placed in media content, may serve to increase the accessibility of the persuasive or commercial intent behind placed brands. The Interactive Advertising Bureau (IAB) as well as, for instance, the U.S. Federal Trade Commission (FTC) and the European Commission, have developed guidelines on how sponsored media content should be disclosed. For instance, the European "television without frontiers" guideline stipulates that the presence of product placement in TV programs is disclosed in advance to the consumer.[1] The FTC states that disclosures on social media (e.g., native advertising and influencer marketing) should be made in the clearest and most conspicuous possible terms that allow the message to be understood as advertising. Disclosures should thus be easily noticed and clearly understood. The FTC therefore imposes using the words or hashtag "sponsored," "ad," or "paid" on all social media advertising messages, on top of the required disclosures that platforms such as Facebook and Instagram impose. For instance, Instagram offers the hashtag "paid partnership with [Brand]" in influencers' post headers.

Nowadays, a particularly sensitive area is influencer marketing for which the FTC additionally developed more detailed (disclosure) rules. For instance, influencers should not lie about their bad experience with a product they disclose. They must disclose any time they are endorsing a product because of a paid partnership or personal affiliation with the brand. That includes family relationships and free products, as well as paid sponsorships. YouTube influencers must put the relationship/ endorsement disclosure in the video description and in the first 30 seconds of the actual video. Instagram influencers should add a disclosure text overlay on their images. Disclosures should appear before "click to read more" buttons appear. Real-time videos (for instance on Snapchat and Instagram stories) should show a prominent superimposed verbal disclosure or text annotation. In live stream videos, the disclosure should be repeated regularly.

Children: a vulnerable target group

One of the most debated ethical issues is advertising to children and teenagers. Children are not only exposed to TV ads and online commercial content, but also to brand placement in movies, apps and games, integrated merchandising plans, and in-school marketing. Sometimes adult products are also targeted at pre-adults (for instance, so-called "alcopops"). Breweries promote their beer brands to college students during spring breaks, festivals, and so on. Companies advertise in and around schools, air commercials during children's programs, target children on product packaging, on point-of-purchase displays, and during sporting events, and place brands in programs targeted at children. Some say that advertising to children is inherently unfair and deceptive because children lack the cognitive skills and life experiences needed to resist persuasive claims and because marketers take advantage of a child's inability to make an informed decision. In other words, they do not have a well-developed persuasion knowledge. *Persuasion knowledge* (sometimes also called *advertising literacy*) implies three types of knowledge: agent knowledge, topic knowledge, and tactic knowledge. *Agent knowledge* describes the beliefs about the goal of the persuasive agent (e.g., the advertiser). *Topic knowledge* is the knowledge the receiver has about the topic of the persuasive message (e.g., knowledge about a product). *Tactic knowledge* describes the knowledge about the persuasive tactics used (e.g., integration or personalization of an advertising message). Persuasion knowledge leads to more in-depth ad processing and coping with the persuasive attempt, for instance by being more critical toward it. In that respect, children have a number of unique vulnerabilities. A new challenge is the integration of advertising and other media content and the enjoyable interactive nature of contemporary advertising formats. TV commercials focus on entertainment and image creation and are often linked to exciting website games (advergames) and brand characters. Brands targeted at children are placed in movies. Commercially sponsored websites contain games and promotions designed for children. Disguising advertising as content or entertainment makes it harder for children to deploy defence mechanisms. This new evolution is an ethical issue because it is potentially misleading by concealing the true nature of the materials and omitting to disclose its commercial intent (Box 6.3). Moreover, parents cannot fully play their role as active mediators of their children's exposure to advertising, because often they do not have the advertising literacy either to fully understand contemporary online advertising, and because children are increasingly exposed to these advertisements on mobile devices, the use of which is hard for parents to monitor.

Box 6.3 Research: advertisers' perceptions of the ethical appropriateness of new advertising formats aimed at children and teenagers

Nowadays, children and teenagers grow up in a predominantly online media environment in which they encounter new integrated and/or interactive advertising formats on a regular basis. A study conducted through an online survey with 95 Belgian advertising professionals tried to explore which new advertising formats are mostly used toward children and teenagers and from which age onward advertisers think: minors understand the commercial intention behind new advertising formats; the usage of these new advertising formats is ethically acceptable; minors should be made aware of the commercial intent of these advertising techniques; and what the characteristics of an ethical data collection and data protection policy are. The participants were invited to provide answers to these questions for each of the nine descriptions of advertising formats: brand placement on television, in-game advertising, advergames, apps, video advertising, merchandising, online behavioral advertising (OBA), search engine marketing, and location-based services.

The most often used advertising formats toward children were contests, branded websites, premiums (a gift in exchange for the purchase of the product), and advergames. Contests, banners, and branded websites were the most often used advertising formats toward teenagers. OBA and location-based services were the least used advertising formats toward both children and teenagers. According to the respondents, the average age at which minors can understand the different advertising formats is around 12–13 years. In-game advertising, product placement, and especially video advertising are considered the most difficult formats to understand. On average, advertising formats are perceived as ethical when targeted at minors from the age of 12–13 years onward. The average age from which minors should be informed about the commercial intent of advertising formats indicated is around 9–10 years.

According to the vast majority of the respondents, a proper data collection and protection policy should provide verification of the age of the children or teenagers, allow verification of the status of the children's or teenagers' parents or legal guardians, and should provide clear information concerning the use of cookies and the possibility of disabling them to children and teenagers. A substantial majority of the respondents agreed that the collection of personal information of children should be prohibited. A majority of the advertisers agreed that children should not be allowed to register on brand websites or mobile platforms without the permission of their parents or legal guardians. If teenagers are considered as a target group the results are mixed (41.1% disagreed and 33.7% agreed). Advertisers think that it is important to notify parents or legal guardians if personal information from their children and teenagers is processed. If children are a target group, collection of personal data was perceived as unethical by the vast majority of advertising professionals. The results for teenagers were mixed (42.1% agreed, 57.9% disagreed). The majority of advertisers also agreed with the statement that parents should give their permission for the data collection of their children and teenagers.

Privacy

Technological developments have given advertisers the opportunity to collect and analyze a massive amount of information about the target audience, and use it in personalized or customized online advertising. Contemporary online advertising formats often have the additional purpose of gathering personal information from the receiver of the advertising message by persuading individuals to disclose their data by having them register or create an account on a website or application. Personal data are also collected by tracking media users' online activities and preferences. These data are then used to develop highly targeted online advertising campaigns. Contemporary online advertising techniques raises a number of privacy concerns: Is it ethical to use information that individuals leave behind online? Which data are collected and how? How (long) are the data stored and used? Who has access to these data? Are they sold to third parties? Can individuals have access to their data and do they have the right to have certain data removed?

A particularly ethically sensitive issue in that respect is "third-party cookies." They are placed by a domain that is different than what is shown in the browser's address bar. Typically, search engines such as Google and many social media place third-party cookies on a network of millions of other sites. This enables them to collect massively more data than they already gather via the first-party cookies on their own platform. Search engines and social networking sites thus gather data about Internet users and provide advertisers with indirect access to these data by serving as intermediaries in the personalization process. Before they are allowed to use any cookies, cookie-hosting websites are legally obligated to communicate all cookie-related information to their visitors and have to ask for their permission regarding the cookie policy to receive their consent. However, by choosing "I Agree" without changing any of the default settings, users usually allow both first-party and third-party cookies to be stored in their web browser. From the point of view of online media users, there is a trade-off between privacy and efficiency (the *privacy calculus*). Customers disclose personal information that is then used by marketers. The more information that is disclosed, the bigger the privacy issue, but also the more efficient advertising becomes in terms of targeting specific audiences and the more relevant the ads that the consumer is exposed to. At the same time, there is the "*privacy paradox*": Individuals self-disclose significant amounts of personal data yet at the same time have either conscious or subconscious concerns about their online privacy. This constitutes a major ethical implication: The result of having to give consent is that individuals act contrary to what they believe (the privacy paradox), especially in the case of immediate gratification for disclosing personal information (e.g., receiving a discount when subscribing to a newsletter). The benefits of having access to the site without seeing the irritating cookie bar or without performing the interruptive act of disabling cookies are also two immediate rewards that trump one's potential privacy concerns.

Table 6.1   GDPR principles

Lawfulness, Fairness, and Transparency	The personal data needs to be processed in a way that is lawful to the subject
Purpose Limitation	The data processors can only use the data for the objectives they've explicitly described and justified
Data Minimization	The information that is required has to be relevant for its purpose and limited to what is necessary
Trueness and Accuracy	If some of the data is inaccurate, it should be removed or rectified
Storage Limitation	Data is kept in a form which permits identification of persons for no longer than is necessary for the purposes for which the personal data is processed
Integrity and Confidentiality	Taking all required measures to ensure all the personal data is protected

What is needed to organize these data collection and usage methods in a more ethical way is increased transparency and increased behavioral control. Increased transparency relates to being honest and open about tracking activities and data handling in such a way that it is understandable for everyone. Increased behavioral control relates to empowering (potential) customers to decide for themselves how they want their data to be collected, stored, processed, exchanged, and used. When doing this correctly, the platform simultaneously informs (potential) customers about what they reveal to the advertiser. While giving (potential) customers more control over their own data, the advertiser makes them more "data literate" for the future as well. Consequently, users might be better skilled to protect their online privacy elsewhere on the Internet.

In 2019, across Europe, the *General Data Protection Regulation* (GDPR) came into force. Any company or individual that processes personal data by which an individual can be identified will also be held responsible for the protection of that data and is responsible for the privacy rights of every person when it comes to collecting and processing their data. Every company who wants to do business in an EU country needs to comply. The principles of the GDPR are summarized in Table 6.1. Non-compliance under the GDPR may bring fines of up to 4% of the company's annual global turnover or €20 million, whichever is higher.

Ethically vulnerable industries

There are a number of specific industries that are particularly vulnerable for ethical issues. For instance, the tourism industry is vulnerable for ethical misbehavior in several ways. Often, the tourism industry does not take into account the good of the destination, which includes recognition of diverse inhabitants and cultural groups, equal respect, and equal dignity of human beings and the ecological footprint of the industry. The fashion industry is a global and complex industry that often does not take the responsibility to raise awareness about consumer materialism, counterfeit fashion consumption, fair trade concerns, social marketing issues, and promotion of impossible lifestyles, among others. The Ethical Fashion Forum defines a number of criteria for ethical fashion: counteract fast fashion and its damaging impact; promote fair wages, working conditions, workers' rights, and ensure sustainable livelihoods; reduction of ecological footprint (avoid harmful substances, such as toxic pesticides, use eco-friendly material, reduce water usage, recycle, incorporate energy efficiency, and support sustainable standards for fashion); raise awareness on ethical behavior; and promote animal rights. Although a number of initiatives have been taken to advance the ethical quality of the fashion industry, the industry still has a lot to do in terms of taking care of these ethical principles.

One trend in the health care industry that has gained importance over recent years is eHealth and mHealth, with important ramifications for ethical communication. *eHealth* is a group of activities that use electronic means to deliver health-related information, resources, and services. *mHealth* is part of eHealth and refers to the use of mobile and wireless technologies to support the achievement of health objectives, for instance, health apps, wearables, and fitness trackers. Concerns have been raised with respect to the quality of information, information transparency, and information asymmetry (patients typically have less information than experts and app developers), digital health literacy (can users understand information and how apps work?), harvesting of personal sensitive data, invasion and loss of privacy, loss of surveillance, control, and human agency (as a result of automation), and fear of data breaches.

There is a whole range of industries that market legal but harmful products when consumed excessively, such as soft drinks, tobacco, alcohol, and confectionery. Advertising has a direct impact on the consumption of these products. Confectionery and soft drinks fail to supply proper nourishment, food cravings occur, and people want to consume more. In conjunction with largely sedentary lifestyles and without enough exercise to counter excessive consumption, obesity and other health-related issues result. The marketing of confectionery and soft drinks has been heavily criticized for its targeting of children, its encouragement of impulse purchases, and for persuading regular consumers to consume larger amounts. Advertising has been found to influence strongly the food preferences of children and is contributing to childhood obesity. Marketing initiatives that target children set them up for a lifetime of bad habits and health problems. With their limited cognitive and emotional processing capacity, children are less able to evaluate critically and resist persuasive communications. Globally, the promotion of confectionery and soft drinks is dominated by television advertising that targets children. Advertisements frequently employ visual, audio, and emotive cues that appeal specifically to children, using fantasy images, fun/humor, and cartoon characters. Online advertising integrated within online social networks is another common strategy for marketing confectionery and soft drinks, and also targets the younger population. This type of advertising frequently employs seamless interaction with consumers through branded games, competition prizes, and giveaways. Advertising messages and packaging labels often suggest that confectionery and soft drink products are actually "healthy" and "balanced." Related to soft drinks, advertising and labeling taglines frequently include "no artificial colors and flavors," reflecting the manufacturers' attempts to enhance a product's perceived "healthiness," while reducing negative health risks associated with consumption.

Like confectionery and soft drinks, bulk buy discounting is also used extensively in alcohol promotion, which stimulates larger purchases and increased consumption. The industry has also come under criticism in relation to advertising that seeks to reduce the perceived risks of alcohol consumption. Labeling beverages as "natural," "gluten free," "no artificial color or flavors," "good for you," as well as using advertising images of natural ingredients and healthy lifestyles, play a significant role in this regard. Alcohol is heavily promoted through social media channels. For instance, an Australia-wide study of Facebook brand marketing in 2014 identified nearly two million fans of the 10 most popular alcohol brands. In 2019, the Facebook alcohol fan base for beer, wine, and spirits grew to over 3.5 million. Similar to confectionery and soft drinks, this type of marketing employs direct interaction and engagement, often via competitions between the social media users that seek to turn them into greater consumers of alcoholic beverages by normalizing daily consumption. Finally, despite bans on tobacco advertising the industry is adept at finding new ways to communicate with customers. These include vulnerable and disadvantaged groups. One recent trend has been an escalation in "influencer" marketing. Regulation has not prevented tobacco advertisers from using social media influencers to post content that promotes their products to young people.

Box 6.4 Practice: Libresse: purpose-based advertising

Purpose-based advertising is defining what a company does beyond making money, and how it can make its customers' lives better. Libresse is a global brand specializing in feminine care – the brand is known for its products for periods. Historically, the intimate care category has been framed as a problem/solution category. It was surrounded by a negative aura and feelings of shame, a cycle that Libresse set out to break. In 2013, Libresse created a global communications platform, Live Fearless, to stimulate women to live the life they want without letting periods hold them back. Libresse wanted to give the brand a point of view, a sense of purpose: give women confidence, and help create the conditions for women to live the life they want, by breaking period and genital taboos. In 2016, Libresse launched RedFit: a campaign that for the first time featured sportswomen bleeding and proudly asserting that "No blood should hold us back."

In 2017, the campaign Bloodnormal was launched. For the first time in the history of femcare, Libresse swapped the infamous blue liquid for red, showed period blood trickling down a woman's leg, a girl publicly asking for a pad, a man buying pads, the emotional journey of periods, the pain, the intimacy, and the beauty. At the end of 2018, Libresse decided to expand into a broader offering of products for women's intimate area. The brand wanted to stay true to Live Fearless and apply its taboo-busting attitude to that category. The "Viva La Vulva" campaign wanted to be a joyous and unashamed ode to the vulva, by means of truthful, positive representations of women's genitals through an infinite diversity of shapes and forms. The campaign was designed to normalize periods and vulvas, and to push the boundaries of representations to be truer than ever to women and their vulva, and overturn a long history of shame and objectification. Viva La Vulva is a lip-sync music video with a twist. It shows a diversity of vulvas of every shape and color singing loud and proud. The film ends on behind-the-scene interviews with women, opening up about the issue, the shame, the ignorance, and reclaiming their bodies.[2]

Released in Scandinavia, the campaign immediately traveled around the world. With no paid media support at all, the Viva la Vulva ad quickly reached over five million organic views and gained 96% positive comments on social media. There was an immediate sales uplift at launch, meeting or surpassing targets across the campaign period.[3]

Self-regulation

On top of legislation and government regulation, in many countries organizations or systems of self-regulation are in place, usually patronized by the advertising community who, in many countries, has regulated its industry by establishing and enforcing codes of practice or sets of guiding principles, a process called self-regulation. Self-regulatory organizations (SROs), which are funded by the advertising industry, ensure that these rules are applied. They all share the same goal: responsible advertising, prepared with a sense of social responsibility to the consumer and society and with proper respect for the rules of fair competition. Due to its flexibility, speed, and low cost, it is generally acknowledged that self-regulation makes an ideal complement to the law.

The most important resource for most SROs worldwide is the *International Chamber of Commerce*'s (ICC) *Advertising and Marketing Communication Code*, first established in 1937. The ICC code puts forward a number of principles that are to be respected in all marketing communication activities: all marketing communications should be legal, decent, honest, and truthful; should be prepared with a due sense of social and professional responsibility; should conform to the principles of fair competition, as generally accepted in business; and no communication should be such as to impair public confidence in marketing. The Code is the global reference point for advertising standards. It is intended primarily as an instrument of advertising self-regulation.

The European Advertising Standards Alliance (EASA) promotes responsible advertising by means of effective self-regulation, while being mindful of national differences in culture, as well as legal and commercial practice. The EASA principles, laid down in a Blue Book, exist in addition to other European and national laws, and are inspired by global (for instance, the ICC code) and local ad standards, codes, or sets of principles that local ad member state ecosystems voluntarily comply with. They are implemented and enforced by the national self-regulatory systems that form EASA's network. EASA members consist of both national SROs and industry associations. In early 2021, the EASA has 27 self-regulation organizations members from 25 European countries and 13 industry associations (advertisers, agencies, and media).

In 2019, the 27-member SROs received 60,682 complaints related to 35,042 ads. These numbers have remained relatively stable during recent years. About 60% of these complaints were filed in the U.K. and a further 15% in Germany; 82% were filed by consumers, 7% by competitors, and 6% by interest groups. Misleading advertising is by far the most important category (58%), followed by taste and decency (18%), and social responsibility (14%). Within the two latter categories, ads allegedly inappropriate to children (25%), gender-related (25%), and other (non-gender) discrimination issues (24%) are the most important categories. As to media, digital advertising accounts for 42% of complaints, followed by audio-visual (28%) and outdoor (7%). The retail industry accounts for 22.5% of complaints, health and beauty for 13%, and leisure services for 11.5%. On average, 38% of the complaints were upheld, 19% were not upheld, and 14% resolved informally. SROs received 96,352 copy advice requests by advertisers of agency (preliminary requests for advice about advertising campaigns to be launched). There were also 332 cross-border complaints.[4]

Ethical responsibility of advertisers, public policy, and education

In order to improve ethical standards and behavior, the advertising industry, governments, and the educational system need to focus more on ethical issues and the implementation or enforcement of ethical behavior.

First of all, companies have to make an effort. Advertising managers need systematically to identify the negative ethical consequences of their strategies and actions. For example, including privacy concerns throughout an innovation process of data-driven services protects against future harmful use of data. Other examples are avoiding stereotypical representation of consumer groups in advertising materials – consider the negative consequences of the "sex sells" notion and exposing individuals to sexualized and objectified images that promote the derogatory treatment of people. Companies might also develop formal codes of conduct and protocols for their advertising activities. They should also include ethical perceptions and considerations in their daily work (e.g., in social media activities) and preparation for extraordinary situations (e.g., in crisis management plans). Companies might also participate in the development of industry schemes or legal regulations to determine ethical standards in advertising practices. Sustainable marketing is still a relatively peripheral concern for marketers – instead of merely avoiding "greenwashing," sustainable marketing needs to become mainstream, and the advertising community has to explore new ways of marketing to make sustainability marketing genuinely transformational.

One of the major ethical challenges is the access that companies have to data that are used to personalize advertising. Since the online tracking industry is evolving at such a high pace, it is impossible for legislators to timely and adequately regulate these practices. Consequently, companies also have the obligation to develop and live by ethical codes of conduct regarding the collection and use of personal data and related privacy issues. Ethical strategies could be increased by means of transparency and increased control by consumers. Additionally, the advertising industry should develop best practices for the appropriate disclosure of all advertising formats, especially with respect to novel online integrated and/or interactive advertising formats (brand placement, native ads …), for instance by developing a clear and uniform cue across media and advertising formats to signal content as advertising. The advertising industry could also develop easy-to-use tools to enable parents to monitor and/or restrict their children's advertising exposure and protect their privacy, and facilitate the development of advertising literacy amongst children, parents, and teachers, for instance by developing or assisting in the development of awareness and educational materials.

There are several areas in which public policy should make (greater) efforts to enforce more ethical marketing practices. One example is protecting children and teenagers. Despite existing public policy initiatives to protect minors against potentially misleading and deceptive advertising, there still exists a lack of regulation on novel and especially online integrated and/or interactive advertising formats, and public policy could do more to impose rules and restrictions on the advertising and media industry to target children and teenagers in a more fair and ethical way. Public policy could also enforce the use of a clear and transparent advertising disclosure cue that is uniform across media and advertising formats. More measures could also be taken to reduce or avoid stereotyping based on gender, ethnicity, or sexual orientation, or the disrespectful portrayal of people in advertising. Given the fast evolution of techniques to collect personal information online and use it for marketing purposes, public policy should continuously monitor and adapt privacy regulations to protect consumers from the harmful consequences of big data-based marketing practices.

Public policy could also contribute to more ethical marketing practices by means of awareness campaigns about advertising tactics and their effects on consumer behavior, that develop knowledge and vigilance with consumers. To enable parents to cope with their children's Internet use and online advertising exposure, it is crucial to develop initiatives to increase parents' advertising literacy. Raising the advertising literacy of parents may be done by means of public policy campaigns, supported by the advertising industry or media, or by organizing workshops, especially for less well-educated parents.

Finally, there are several areas in which the education system plays a crucial role in developing sensitivities and skills that can lead to a more ethical advertising practice. Primary and secondary schools should develop educational materials on advertising literacy and use them in the classroom. Also teachers and policymakers should be educated about how contemporary advertising formats work and why these advertising formats are effective. Additionally, it is important to properly educate business school students to develop genuine knowledge about ethics and develop ethical attitudes and behavior in business and marketing practice. The reinforcement of ethical dimensions in all course modules is important – failure to do so may send a signal that ethics is not, in fact, operationally important.[5]

Notes

1. https://ec.europa.eu/commission/presscorner/detail/en/MEMO_06_419.
2. https://www.youtube.com/watch?v=0k-_4WloY6Y.
3. Tanja Grubner (ESSITY GMBH); Margaux Revol, Bridget Angear (AMV BBDO); https://www.essity.com/.
4. https://www.easa-alliance.org/sites/default/files/EASA%20Complaints%20Annual%20Report%202019.pdf.
5. An extensive overview and discussion of ethical issues in marketing and advertising can be found in L. Eagle, S. Dahl, P. De Pelsmacker, and C.R. Taylor (eds.) (2021), *The Sage Handbook of Marketing Ethics*, Sage.

Suggested further reading

Ajzen, I. (2002). Perceived behavioral control, self-efficacy, locus of control, and the theory of planned behavior. *Journal of Applied Social Psychology, 32*(4), 665–83.

Aleksandrovs, L., Goos, P., Dens, N., & De Pelsmacker, P. (2015). Mixed-media modeling may help optimize campaign recognition and brand interest: how to apply the "mixture-amount modeling" method to cross-platform effectiveness measurement. *Journal of Advertising Research, 55*(4), 443–57.

Andrews, J.C. & Shimp, T.A. (2017). *Advertising, Promotion, and Other Aspects of Integrated Marketing Communications* (10th edn.). Cengage.

Ang, L. (2021). *Principles of Integrated Marketing Communications: An Evidence-Based Approach* (2nd edn.). Cambridge University Press.

Ang, S.H., Lee, Y.H., & Leong, S.M. (2007).The ad creativity cube: conceptualization and initial validation. *Journal of the Academy of Marketing Science, 35*(2), 220–32.

Avramova, Y., Dens, N., & De Pelsmacker, P. (2021). Brand placement across media: the interaction of placement modality and frequency in film versus text. *Journal of Business Research, 128*, 20–30.

Bagozzi, R.P., Gopinath, M., & Nyer, P.U. (1999). The role of emotions in marketing. *Journal of the Academy of Marketing Science, 27*(2), 184–206.

Banks, I.B., De Pelsmacker, P., & Okazaki, S. (eds.) (2014). *Advances in Advertising Research (vol. V): Extending the Boundaries of Advertising.* Springer.

Buzeta, C., Dens, N., & De Pelsmacker, P. (2020). Motivations to use different social media types and their impact on consumers' online brand-related activities (COBRAs). *Journal of Interactive Marketing, 52*, 79–98.

Cauberghe, V., De Pelsmacker, P., Janssens, W., & Dens, N. (2009). Fear, threat and efficacy in threat appeals: message involvement as a key mediator to message acceptance. *Accident Analysis and Prevention, 41*(2), 276–85.

Chaiken, S. (1980). Heuristic versus systematic information processing in the use of source versus message cues in persuasion. *Journal of Personality and Social Psychology, 39*, 752–66.

Cheng, H. (ed.) (2014). *The Handbook of International Advertising Research.* John Wiley & Sons.

Cialdini, R.B. (2009). *Influence: Science and Practice* (5th edn.). Pearson.

Colicev, A., Malshe, A., Pauwels, K., & O'Connor, P. (2018). Improving consumer mindset metrics and shareholder value through social media: the different roles of owned and earned media. *Journal of Marketing, 82*(1), 37–56.

Daems, K., De Pelsmacker, P., & Moons, I. (2017). Advertisers' perceptions regarding the ethical appropriateness of new advertising formats aimed at minors. *Journal of Marketing Communications, 25*(4), 438–56.

Daems, K., De Pelsmacker, P., & Moons, I. (2019). The effect of integration and interactivity on young teenagers' memory, brand attitude and personal data sharing. *Computers in Human Behavior, 99*, 245–59.

De Keyzer, F., Dens, N., & De Pelsmacker, P. (2019). The impact of relational characteristics on responses to word of mouth on social network sites. *International Journal of Electronic Commerce, 23*(2), 212–43.

De Keyzer, F., Dens, N., & De Pelsmacker, P. (2021). How and when personalized advertising leads to Brand Attitude, Click and WOM Intention. *Journal of Advertising*, DOI: 10.1080/00913367.2021.1888339.

De Meulenaer, S., Dens, N., De Pelsmacker, P., & Eisend, M. (2018). How consumers' values influence responses to male and female gender role stereotyping in advertising. *International Journal of Advertising, 37*(6), 893–913.

De Pelsmacker, P. (ed.) (2016). *Advertising in New Formats and Media: Current Research and Implications for Marketers*. Emerald.

De Pelsmacker, P., Dens, N., & Verberckmoes, S. (2019). How ad congruity and interactivity affect fantasy game players' attitude toward in-game advertising. *Journal of Electronic Commerce Research, 20*(1), 55–74.

De Pelsmacker, P., Geuens, M., & Van den Bergh, J. (2021). *Marketing Communications: A European Perspective*. Pearson.

Dens, N., De Pelsmacker, P., & Verhellen, Y. (2018). Better together? Harnessing the power of brand placement through program sponsorship messages. *Journal of Business Research, 83*, 151–9.

Dens, N., De Pelsmacker, P., Wouters, M., & Purnawirawan, N. (2012). Do you like what you recognize? The effects of brand placement prominence and movie plot connection on brand attitude as mediated by recognition. *Journal of Advertising, 41*(3), 35–54.

Dillard, J.P. & Shen, L. (2005). On the nature of reactance and its role in persuasive communication. *Communication Monographs, 72*(2), 144–68.

Eagle, L., Dahl, S., De Pelsmacker, P., & Taylor, C.R. (eds.) (2021). *The Sage Handbook of Marketing Ethics*. Sage.

Eisend, M., Langner, T., & Okazaki, S. (eds.) (2012). *EAA Advances in Advertising Research (vol. III)*. Springer.

Eisend, M., van Reijmersdal, E.A., Boerman, S.C., & Tarrahi, F. (2020). A meta-analysis of the effects of disclosing sponsored content. *Journal of Advertising, 49*(3), 344–66.

Fisher, N.I. & Kordupleski, R.E. (2019). Good and bad market research: a critical review of Net Promoter Score. *Applied Stochastic Models in Business and Industry, 35*(1), 138–51.

Forgas, J.P. (1995). Mood and judgment: the Affect Infusion Model (AIM). *Psychological Bulletin, 117*(1), 39–66.

Friestad, M. & Wright, P. (1994). The persuasion knowledge model: how people cope with persuasion attempts. *Journal of Consumer Research, 21*(June), 1–31.

Frijda, N.H. (1987). *The Emotions*. Cambridge University Press.

Gyygli, S., Haelg, F., Potrafke, N., & Sturm, J.-E. (2019). The KOF Globalisation Index – revisited. *Review of International Organizations, 14*(3), 543–74.

Hennig-Thurau, T., Hofacker, C., & Bloching, B. (2013). Marketing the pinball way: understanding how social media change the generation of value for consumers and companies. *Journal of Interactive Marketing, 27*, 237–41.

Hoyer, W.C., MacInnis, D.J., & Pieters, R. (2018). *Consumer Behavior* (7th edn.). Cengage.

Hughes, C., Swaminathan, V., & Brooks, G. (2019). Driving brand engagement through online social influencers: an empirical investigation of sponsored blogging campaigns. *Journal of Marketing, 83*(5), 78–96.

Kahneman, D. (2011). *Thinking, Fast and Slow*. Farrar, Straus and Giroux.

Keller, K.L. & Swaminathan, V. (2019). *Strategic Brand Management: Building, Measuring, and Managing Brand Equity (Global Edition)*. Pearson.

Kotler, P. & Keller K.L. (2015). *Marketing Management*. Pearson.

Laudon, K.C. & Traver, C.G. (2019). *E-commerce 2018: Business, Technology, Society*. Pearson.

Lee, J.A. & Usunier, J.C. (2013). *Marketing Across Cultures* (6th edn.). Pearson.

Lipschultz, J.H. (2020). *Social Media Communication* (3rd edn.). Routledge.

Okazaki, S. (ed.) (2012). *Handbook of Research on International Advertising*. Edward Elgar Publishing.

Petty, R.E. & Cacioppo, J.T. (1986). The elaboration likelihood model of persuasion. *Advances in Experimental Social Psychology, 19*, 123–205.

Pham, M.T., Geuens, M., & De Pelsmacker, P. (2013). The influence of ad-evoked feelings on brand evaluations: empirical generalizations from consumer responses to more than 1000 TV commercials. *International Journal of Research in Marketing, 30*(4), 383–94.

Rajabi, M., Dens, N., De Pelsmacker, P., & Goos, P. (2017). Consumer responses to different degrees of advertising adaptation: the moderating role of national openness to foreign markets. *International Journal of Advertising, 36*(2), 293–313.

Ries, A. & Trout, J. (2001). *Positioning: The Battle for Your Mind* (2nd edn.). McGraw-Hill.

Rodgers, S.L. & Thorson, E.L. (eds.) (2017). *Digital Advertising*. Routledge.

Rodgers, S.L. & Thorson, E.L. (eds.) (2019). *Advertising Theory* (2nd edn.). Routledge.

Rosengren, S., Dahlen, M., & Okazaki, S. (eds.) (2013). *Advances in Advertising Research (vol. IV)*. Springer.

Smit, E.G., Van Noort, G., & Voorveld, H.A. (2014). Understanding online behavioural advertising: user knowledge, privacy concerns and online coping behaviour in Europe. *Computers in Human Behavior, 32*, 15–22.

van Reijmersdal, E.A. & Rozendaal, E. (2020). Transparency of digital native and embedded advertising: opportunities and challenges for regulation and education, *Communications: The European Journal of Communication Research, 45*(3), 378–88.

Vaughn, R. (1986). How advertising works: a planning model revisited. *Journal of Advertising Research, 26*(1), 57–66.

Verhellen, Y., Dens, N., & De Pelsmacker, P. (2013). A longitudinal content analysis of gender role portrayal in Belgian television advertising. *Journal of Marketing Communications, 22*(2), 170–88.

Verhellen, Y., Eelen, J., Dens, N., & De Pelsmacker, P. (2015). The short- and long-term impact of brand placement in an Advertiser Funded Program on viewers' attitudes towards the sponsor brand and its main competitor. *International Journal of Advertising, 35*(6), 932–48.

Verlegh, P., Voorveld, H., & Eisend, M. (eds.) (2016). *Advances in Advertising Research (vol. VI).* Springer.

Witte, K. (1994). Fear control and danger control: a test of the extended parallel process model (EPPM). *Communication Monographs, 61,* 113–34.

Online resources

http://www.iab.net/media/file/IAB-Native-Advertising-Playbook2.pdf.
https://adespresso.com/blog/influencer-marketing-guidelines/.
https://ads.tiktok.com.
https://blog.hollywoodbranded.com.
https://blog.hubspot.com/marketing/how-to-do-a-b-testing.
https://blogs.constantcontact.com/facebook-call-to-action-button/.
https://businessjargons.com/marketing-communication.
https://business.linkedin.com/marketing-solutions/ads/pricing?#.
https://business.linkedin.com/marketing-solutions/how-to-advertise-on
-linkedin.
https://business.twitter.com/en/advertising/campaign-types.html.
https://collectivelyinc.com/blog/industry-insights/rules-for-brands-and
-influencers-to-be-ftc-compliant.
http://contentmarketinginstitute.com.
https://contentmarketinginstitute.com/2008/11/purpose-based-marketing-jim
-stengel-and-content-marketing/.
https://conversionsciences.com/facebook-ads-simplified-tofu/.
https://cxl.com/blog/cialdinis-principles-persuasion/.
https://digiday.com/media/what-is-programmatic-advertising/.
https://exploringyourmind.com/the-affect-infusion-model-mood-and
-judgment/.
https://geomarketing.com/geomarketing-101-what-is-geo-targeting.
https://hi.hofstede-insights.com.
https://help.pinterest.com/en/business/guide/becoming-an-advertiser-on
-pinterest.
https://iccwbo.org/content/uploads/sites/3/2018/09/icc-advertising-and
-marketing-communications-code-int.pdf.
https://influencermarketinghub.com/how-much-do-youtube-ads-cost/.
https://influencermarketinghub.com/how-to-advertise-on-snapchat/.
https://itlaw.wikia.org/wiki/online_behavioral_advertising#cite_note-0.
https://kotlermarketing.com.
https://later.com/blog/paid-partnership-feature/.
https://marketingmix.co.uk.

https://medium.com/inside-revenue/how-do-i-target-audiences-on-snapchat-part-2-76f0c048e453.

https://multimediamarketing.com/mkc/marketingcommunications/.

https://neilpatel.com/what-is-facebook-advertising/.

https://neilpatel.com/what-is-google-adwords/.

https://support.google.com/google-ads/.

https://themanifest.com/mobile-apps/how-app-advertising-works-app-monetization.

https://vwo.com/ab-testing/.

https://www.aai.ie/resources/uploads/Glossary_of_Advertising_Terms.pdf.

https://www.ama.org.

https://www.bigcommerce.com/blog/social-media-advertising/#what-are-the-benefits-of-advertising-on-social-media-channels.

http://www.brandstories.net.

https://www.brandwatch.com/.

https://www.brightedge.com/glossary/benefits-recommendations-ab-testing.

https://www.digitalmarketer.com/blog/youtube-ad-types/.

http://www.easa-alliance.org/.

https://www.economicsdiscussion.net/advertising/definitions-of-advertising.

https://www.exchangewire.com/blog/2019/12/18/predictions-2020-the-rise-of-contextual-advertising/.

https://www.exin.com/article/6-basic-principles-gdpr?language_content_entity=en.

https://www.facebook.com/business.

https://www.facebook.com/business/ads/ad-targeting.

https://www.forbes.com/sites/louiscolumbus/2018/01/18/analytics-are-defining-the-future-of-digital-advertising/#74508614786f.

https://www.hofstede-insights.com/product/compare-countries/.

https://www.iab.com/guidelines/iab-measurement-guidelines/.

https://www.investopedia.com/terms/a/affiliate-marketing.asp.

https://www.investopedia.com/terms/v/viral-marketing.asp.

https://www.lotame.com/what-is-a-data-management-platform/.

http://www.mcngmarketing.com/how-to-advertise-on-pinterest/.

https://www.mobindustry.net/how-to-monetize-your-app-with-mobile-ads-and-not-fail/.

https://www.optimizely.com/optimization-glossary/ab-testing/.

https://www.politico.eu/article/cambridge-analytica-leave-eu-ukip-brexit-facebook.

https://www.socialmediaexaminer.com/3-ways-to-advertise-on-twitter/.

https://www.socialmediaexaminer.com/how-to-advertise-tiktok/.

https://www.theguardian.com/fashion/2021/mar/10/is-sex-the-best-way-to-sell-suits-when-were-still-social-distancing.

https://www.weidert.com/whole_brain_marketing_blog/bid/113688/ToFu-MoFu-BoFu-Serving-Up-The-Right-Content-for-Lead-Nurturing.

https://www.wired.com/amp-stories/cambridge-analytica-explainer/.

https://www.youtube.com/ads/how-it-works/.

Index

Titles in the **Elgar Advanced Introductions** series include:

International Political Economy
Benjamin J. Cohen

The Austrian School of Economics
Randall G. Holcombe

Cultural Economics
Ruth Towse

Law and Development
*Michael J. Trebilcock and Mariana
Mota Prado*

International Humanitarian Law
Robert Kolb

International Trade Law
Michael J. Trebilcock

Post Keynesian Economics
J.E. King

International Intellectual Property
Susy Frankel and Daniel J. Gervais

Public Management and
Administration
Christopher Pollitt

Organised Crime
Leslie Holmes

Nationalism
Liah Greenfeld

Social Policy
Daniel Béland and Rianne Mahon

Globalisation
Jonathan Michie

Entrepreneurial Finance
Hans Landström

International Conflict and Security
Law
Nigel D. White

Comparative Constitutional Law
Mark Tushnet

International Human Rights Law
Dinah L. Shelton

Entrepreneurship
Robert D. Hisrich

International Tax Law
Reuven S. Avi-Yonah

Public Policy
B. Guy Peters

The Law of International
Organizations
Jan Klabbers

International Environmental Law
Ellen Hey

International Sales Law
Clayton P. Gillette

Corporate Venturing
Robert D. Hisrich

Public Choice
Randall G. Holcombe

Private Law
Jan M. Smits

Consumer Behavior Analysis
Gordon Foxall

Behavioral Economics
John F. Tomer